THE WONDERS OF VILAYET

THE WONDERS OF VILAYET

Being the Memoir, Originally in Persian, of a Visit to France and Britain

MIRZA SHEIKH I'TESAMUDDIN

Translated by Kaiser Haq

PEEPAL TREE

First published in Great Britain in 2001
Reprinted in this new edition 2018
Peepal Tree Press Ltd
17 King's Avenue
Leeds LS6 1QS
England

ISBN 9781900715157

CONTENTS

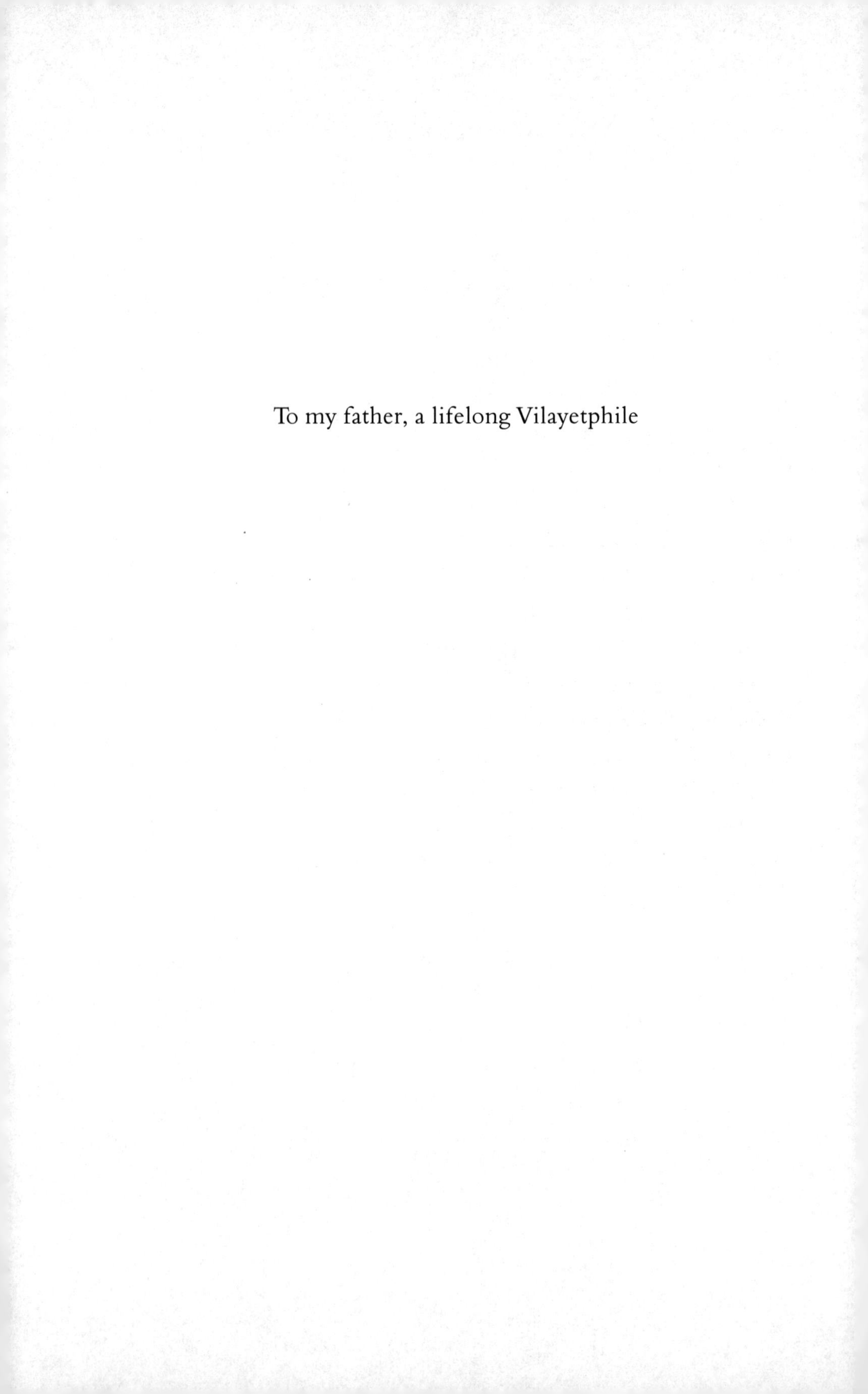

To my father, a lifelong Vilayetphile

THE WONDERS OF VILAYET

TRANSLATOR'S INTRODUCTION

This is the first complete English version of one of the earliest accounts of the modern West by a non-Westerner. I say 'modern' in contradistinction to the medieval West, which had come under the observation of Arab writers. All accounts of 'Otherness' are significant, but 'modern' ones naturally possess an added relevance for us. This being the age of Western expansion and dominance the latter are mostly Western works about the non-Western world. Analysis of these, now a sizeable critical industry, invariably reveals their collusion with colonialism. The thesis is valid in the main, but excessive preoccupation with it may prove to be chiefly an outlet for resentments inherited by the post-colonial intellectual. The aim of healthier relations between peoples, which presumably underlies such critical inquiry, will surely be better served if accounts of 'Otherness' are considered in a dialogic perspective. At least one critic has voiced the need for this. 'I would have liked to learn more about the images of "races" other than the black – the yellow, for example, or the white as seen by nonwhites,' Tzvetan Todorov noted in commenting on contributions to a symposium.[1] Much of the literature about the West by non-Westerners, like the present work, awaits discovery or rediscovery. Opportunities lie here for both publishers and critics.

As often happens with out-of-way literature my introduction to this work occurred quite fortuitously, when in the course of a meandering conversation an old schoolmate declared that an ancestor of his had been the first Indian to visit Britain. The claim, I was to discover, was not to be taken literally. The earliest Indians to reach Europe were probably lascars, but they didn't count, being illiterate and hence unable to leave literary traces of their extraordinary lives. It is generally believed that the first Indian to visit Britain and write about it was the great social reformer Raja Ram Mohun Roy, who spent the last two years of his life (1831-33) there, but my friend's great-great-great-great-granduncle, Mirza Sheikh I'tesamuddin, preceded him by over half a century

In 1765, after granting the revenue rights of Bengal in perpetuity to the East India Company, the Moghul Emperor Shah Alam II, beleaguered as he was by tenacious enemies, implored the protection of His Britannic Majesty's troops. Since it was not in Robert Clive's power to place British soldiers in the service of a foreign court it was agreed that a letter containing the request would be despatched, together with a present of 100,000 rupees from the Emperor to his British counterpart. The Mission was entrusted to Captain Swinton and at the Emperor's suggestion that an Indian well-versed in Persian should be there so that the letter's contents could be properly explicated and interpreted, Mirza Sheikh I'tesamuddin was chosen to accompany him.

Thus began an extraordinary adventure for the Mirza that lasted nearly three years and provided material for a fascinating memoir, though nothing came of the mission. After three weeks at sea the Mirza learned from Captain Swinton that Clive had held back the letter, saying that there was no point in sending it with them as the present intended to accompany it hadn't yet arrived from the Emperor. Clive had promised Captain Swinton that he would himself follow with both the letter and the money and catch up with them in England. But in England the Mirza discovered that Clive had suppressed the letter and presented the money on his own behalf. The reason for such duplicity was that Clive felt, with good reason, that it was in the Company's interest to prevent any direct contact between the English King and the Moghul Emperor.

Had the mission been successful Indian history probably, and this memoir certainly, would have turned out rather differently. India's fortunes might have fared better and the memoir would have given us a close view of the court of George III, but I think the loss is more than made up by the account of the Mirza's travels in Britain, which he might not have been able to undertake if he had become embroiled in diplomatic activities.

It is necessary to look closely at the Mirza's background for us to appreciate the distinctiveness of his memoir. Enough of it is included in the text, but I can add a few more details culled from a private printed Family History by one of his descendants. The likely dates of his birth and death are 1730 and 1800 respectively. The Mirza's family claimed descent from the Prophet Mohamed. The claim may or may not be valid. India is littered with *Sayyids*: the word, meaning simply 'Mister' in Arabic, is used as surname by those who believe they are descended from the Prophet. But we do have the Mirza's family tree, which goes back to the sixteenth century, and we also know that his ancestors came to India to escape a Mongol invasion of Persia. The family distinguished itself for piety and scholarship, and its scions never lacked respectable employment in the administration and the judiciary. The Mirza's elder brother was a Mufti, or adviser on Moslem law, to Nawab Alivardi Khan, independent ruler of Bengal from 1740 to 1756. It was Alivardi's successor, his grandson Siraj-ud-dowla, who was defeated at Plassey in 1757. He was replaced by his uncle Mir Jafar, whose name has become the Bengali equivalent of Quisling because of his treacherous role at Plassey; he in turn was supplanted in 1760 by his son-in-law, Mir Kasim, whose ineffectual campaign against the East India Company is recounted in this memoir.

We are told that the Mirza completed his education under Munshi Salimullah, who was employed at Mir Jafar's court. The instruction prepared him for the career of *munshi*, which means 'clerk', of 'scribe', but in those days referred to a more exalted position than it does today. A *munshi* was a scholar whose knowledge of Persian, then the official language, was indispensable in the fields of administration, diplomacy and the law. Officials of the East India Company, we may recall, were required to have some Persian and Hindustani. Most of the Mirza's life as a munshi was spent in the Company's employ, but its high point was the brief spell during which he worked for Emperor Shah Alam II. The Emperor conferred on him the title of Mirza, roughly comparable to a knighthood, thus elevating him to the status of a courtier.

On his return from Europe the Mirza became a local celebrity and was given the nickname of 'Vilayet Munshi', Vilayet being the Indian word for Britain and Europe. During his second stint in the Company's employ he was involved in the diplomatic manoeuvres that ended several years of warfare with the Mahrattas. He began writing his memoir, he tells us, at the behest of friends, and to seek distraction from the anarchy all around. This is no doubt an allusion to the war in South India between the Company and Tipu Sultan. He wrote in Persian, the language he knew best, titling his narrative *Shigurf Nama-e-Vilayet*, or 'Wonderful Tales About Europe'.

He has also left behind a Persian *Nasabnama*, or genealogical compilation, which is the chief source of the Family History mentioned above. Portions quoted in translation or summarised in the latter reveal a pre-occupation with pedigree:

> Although it is not in good taste to some wise people to mention these facts, there are many old fools and impudent young men who, on account of their ignorance or pride of wealth, mistake their impertinence for courage, and their abusive tongue for plain speaking, and without bringing down their heads into the calm mood of thinking they begin disgracing and humiliating people in the open *majlis* [assembly] and in the streets and markets, and engage in debates and disputes, leading gradually to fights and enmities; and, forgetting the calls of kinship, friendship and good neighbourliness and the needs of unity, they abuse the ancestors of one another by saying whatever comes uppermost to their lips; and it is therefore a necessity that the correct facts should be known.[2]

The Mirza took very seriously the Prophet Mohamed's saying that 'One who marries for the sake of wealth debases himself, and one who marries for the sake of beauty disgraces himself, but one who married for lineage and for purity of blood earns the blessings of God.' The Mirza took cryptographic steps 'to indicate the exact quality of blood in the issue of marriages'. He used 'certain signs against the names concerned'; these were Arabic letters, 'such as "Mim" for the people of the Mozaray or the cultivating class, "Ha" for the converted Hindu, "Nun" for widowed girls, "Ayen" for illicit love, "Kaf" for maid servants, "Fay" for prostitutes and "Zay" for connections out of wedlock, etc.etc.'[3]

The mirza, then, was an Indian gentleman, proud of his lineage, well educated in the traditional manner, who happened to live through the most crucial transition in Indian history. When he was born the

East India Company was one among several European trading houses; when he died they were the effective rulers of most of India. Yet he was not, we must remember, a 'colonial subject', and this coupled with his elite background makes his memoir unique. He embodies the humane qualities as well as the prejudices of his culture. He is curious about alien cultures, and is a good observer possessed with an engaging descriptive ability. In this he is a refreshing contrast to the introversion that, as V.S. Naipaul points out in relation to Gandhi, often characterises the colonial subject's response to the West. Equally noteworthy is his comparison of Europe with India, which includes a clear-sighted critique of Indian decadence and a generous acknowledgement of the qualities which have contributed towards European, especially British, ascendancy. His prejudices can be quite embarrassing, and his observations are often skewed by lack of scientific knowledge, but such flaws – especially the latter – generally add a delightful piquancy to the narrative, as do his foibles, like his obsession with *halal* food. Similarly, it is amusing to note how he absorbs the British prejudice against the French.

The reader is bound to be struck by what we may call his sense of race. It is worth pointing out that he belongs to a culture with the longest history of colour prejudice. Aryan hordes pouring into India from the second millennium BC latched on the superficial traits differentiating them from the autochthons as indices of human worth. The 'twice-born' Aryan of the higher castes was light-complexioned and sharp-featured, the 'inferior' low-caste or caste-less Untouchable dark, blunt-featured, shorter. Despite the inevitable racial intermingling down the centuries colour prejudice persists – and colours the sexual aesthetics of most Indians. None is more aware of subtle differences of shade than the Indian. Advertisements today in Indian papers putting up maidens in the marriage market cannot ignore colour: there are the 'fair' cynosures, followed by the 'wheaten complexioned', and if the commodity should be 'dark' the best that can be done is to add '... but attractive'. The Moslem invasions bringing in Arab, Persian, Afghan and Moghul – all lighter-complexioned than the average Indian – reinforced the prejudice, despite the professed egalitarianism of Islam.

The Mirza's comments on the darker peoples encountered on the way reveal his prejudice, as does his ecstatic celebration of European womanhood. The White Woman seems to embody the Platonic idea of beauty; she is a paradisal houri. To our amusement admiration turns to awe in the encounter with the giantess, who in the Mirza's eyes is not a freak of nature, but a Superwoman, Interestingly, we find his feelings echoed a century later in *Les Fleurs du Mal*:

> J'eusse aimé, vivre auprès d'une jeune géante,
> Comme aux pieds d'une reine un chat voluptueux.
>
> J'eusse aimé voir son corps fleurir avec son âme
> Et grandir librement dans ses terribles jeux;
> Deviner si son coeur couve une sombre flamme
> Aux humides brouillards qui nagent dans ses yeux;
>
> Parcourir à loisir ses magnifiques formes;
> Ramper sur le versant de ses genoux énormes,
> Et Parfois en été, quand les soleils malsains,
>
> Lasse, la font s'étendre a travers la compagne,
> Dormir nonchalamment à l'ombre de ses seins,
> Comme un hameau paisible au pied d'une montague.
>
> ('La Géante')

Is it too fanciful to postulate on the basis of this a spiritual kinship between our Mirza, a stranger from the East, and Baudelaire, a native-born Outsider?

The Mirza's original text has never been published. The book that introduced me to him was a complete Bengali translation, *Vilayetnama*, on 'Tales of Vilayet' (Dhaka: Muktadhara, 1981), by the late Professor A.B.M. Habibullah, who had a distinguished career as a teacher of Islamic History in universities in India, Bangladesh and Australia. In a brief preface Professor Habibullah mentions that his translation is based on the two extant manuscripts of the original, one of which is in the British Museum, the other in the Khoda Buksh Library in the town of Bankipur, in Bihar, India. An earlier – 'abridged and flawed' – translation in English by James Edward Alexander, an old India hand, had been published in London in 1827 by John

Taylor under the elaborate title of *Shigurf Namah - i - Vilaet or Excellent Intelligence Concerning Europe, Being the Travels of Mirza Itesa Modeen*. Professor Habibullah identified the portrait of the Mirza which had been reproduced as the book's frontispiece as the work of Northcote, R. A. In 1939 at a conference of the Indian Historical Records Commission Professor Habibullah presented an English translation of the Moghul Emperor's letter to George III, which had somehow survived.

During a Fulbright year in America I obtained a photocopy of Alexander's translation, and finding its style too quaint for modern taste, partly the result of the translator's misguided attempt to capture the peculiarities of Persian syntax, I resolved to produce a more readable English version. My Persian unfortunately did not extend beyond a few words and a certain familiarity with the script acquired through the enforced reading of the Koran (without understanding it) which is part of a Moslem upbringing in the subcontinent,

But I realised that working from the Bengali translation I could remain true to the substance of the original, for seven centuries of Moslem rule in India had introduced the conceptual currency of Persian into the Indian vernaculars. Bengali, especially what some call its 'Islamized' form, is quite capable of capturing the content and emotional tone of Persian.

Though abridged, Alexander's translation has a few extra passages, among them the Invocation and, in Chapter VII, the account of the giantess, some of the details of the riding show and the theatre, and the detailed list of the exhibits in the British Museum. Since these parts are in keeping with the rest there is no reason to doubt their authenticity, and I have included them after editing them in the interests of lucidity. Their existence leads one to believe there were at least two versions of the original text. I have not hesitated to use some scattered lines and phrases from Alexander and have also followed him in identifying Dover, which the Mirza doesn't mention by name, and Nantes and Ascension, whose names he gets wrong. The chapter divisions and titles are mine; the sectional titles within them the Mirza's. I have transposed some parts for the sake of the structure, and to spare the reader unnecessary puzzlement I have deleted reference to an obviously fictional region called Angriya, somewhere 'near Jedda and Basra', whose inhabitants were notorious pirates till an

English fleet put them out of occupation. The Mirza seems to have confused the name of a region which I have failed to identify. Such textual problems, however, need not detain us; the Persian scholar is welcome to while away a sabbatical on them.

I must acknowledge several debts of gratitude: to Kazi Ashfaq, who introduced me to his illustrious ancestor;

Dr Parween Hasan, who helped with the explicatory notes, which for the reader's convenience have been included parenthetically in the text; to David Dabydeen, who has given this work a welcome place in the Warwick University Studies in Asian Migration, and to Jeremy Poynting of the Peepal Tree Press, which has undertaken to publish it. As always my late wife, Dipa, was most supportive.

– Kaiser Haq

Notes

1. Henry Louis Gates, Jr., ed. *Race, Writing and Difference*, Chicago and London: University of Chicago, 1986. p. 377.
2. Qazi Mohamed Sadrul Ola, *History of the Family of Mirza Sheikh I'tesamuddin* (Calcutta 1944, Dhaka 1984), p. iii-iv.
3. Ibid., p. iii.

AN INVOCATION...

In the name of the most beneficent and merciful Allah, to whom all praise is due, who created all there is, rescued the sons of our first parent from the darkness of ignorance, presented them with the splendour of wisdom, made apparent the distinction between good and evil, and in the series of the descendants of Adam finally produced our Prophet, Mohammed. Blessing and peace be upon that chosen Prophet, his illustrious offspring, and his venerable associates, the Caliphs Abu Bakr. Omar, Osman and Ali.

.....AND A PREFACE

Fate took me to Vilayet some years back. An account of my strange experiences on sea and land ought to be entertaining and educative, if I weren't sadly lacking in literary ability. In this year of the Hegira 1199 (1784 A.D.), as the unrest and anarchy all around makes me anxious, distressed and often so upset as to deprive me of reason, it is only at the insistence of friends that I, Sheikh I'tesamuddin, son of late Tajuddin of Panchnoor village in the Nadia district of Bengal, take up pen and paper to inscribe my impressions of the visit. I have used a very plain and restrained style, for I believe jugglery with words is a sign of the misuse of language and of intellectual self-indulgence.

But alas! I am so deficient in intelligence and judgement that I cannot present my observations and ideas in neat and attractive language, and therefore must relinquish any hope of winning the commendation of discerning readers. All I can leave as a mark on the pages of time, by which I may be remembered, is this account of a few curious incidents.

CHAPTER I:

BACKGROUND, PERSONAL AND HISTORICAL

During the reign of Nawab Mir Zafar Ali Khan I had the good fortune to learn to read and write Persian from Mirza Mohammed Kassim, Head Munshi to the Nawab, and Munshi Sheikh Salimullah. After Mir Kassim Ali Khan became Nawab I entered the service of Major Park, and was present during his campaign against Asadussaman, ruler of Birbhum. After the cessation of hostilities I accompanied my employer to Azimabad, where I had the honour of an audience with Badshah Shah Alam, and then to Calcutta, where I joined the seven other Munshis then in the Company's employ. When Major Park returned to England he sent me with a reference to Major Adam at Patna, but owing to the intrigues of Munshi Nabakissan (who now sports the title of Raja), I found no employment. Subsequently, with Mr. Strachey's help I got a job under Captain Mackinon as paymaster of an orphanage. I stayed there two years, after which, in the war that broke out between the Company and Nawab Mir Kassim, I accompanied my employer on his campaign and was present at the battles of Gheria and Udainala. Then for a year I served as *Tahsildar* [tax-collector] of Kutubpur under Mr. Bardette.

Mr. Strachey, who had lent me generous support in my career, suddenly died. I was utterly bereft at the loss of this kind man and for a month I wore a tearful countenance; even now when I remember him I am overcome with sorrow.

Shortly after, in the autumn of 1764, Major Hector Munro trounced the combined forces of Mir Kassim and Shuja-ud-doula at the battle of Baksar, and the latter fled to Rohilkund. In 1765 I took service under the British Commander-in-Chief, Colonel Carnac and had the honour of an audience with the Emperor Shah Alam at Jahajgarh. From there I went to Lucknow by way of Allahabad.

Fresh troubles ensued when Shujauddowla joined hands with the Mahratta Chief Malhar Rao against the Emperor Shah Alam. Shujauddowla advanced to Kulpi and Malhar Rao attacked Kora-Jahanabad with 50,000 horsemen. Colonel Carnac, who was ordered to aid the Emperor, marched from Faizabad. He crossed the Ganges, and engaged the enemy at Sheora-Shahpur ghat, putting them to flight. Malhar Rao fled towards Kulpi, and Shujauddowla towards Kanauj. The stage was set for a peace settlement. Both Shujauddowla and the Emperor proceeded for the purpose to Allahabad, as did yours truly with Colonel Carnac. A sudden turn in my career occurred when we met up with the Emperor at Kora-Manikpur. I was offered a position as Munshi, with the title of Mirza, at the Emperor's Court, which I gratefully accepted.

After my European sojourn I returned to the Company's employ and was involved in the diplomatic manoeuvres connected with the Maratha wars. In 1775 I accompanied Colonel John Hamilton when he went to Poona to conclude a treaty with the Maratha warlords. In the ensuing negotiations I had to act as emissary to the Marathas and, after discussion with the chief Maratha officials, Narad Sakharam and Nana Fadnavis, and with the assistance of Captain Vansittart, draw up the treaty, a copy of which is still in my possession.

In sum, the best part of my youth was spent in the Company's service. Amidst my present misfortune those days seem to me all the more fortunate.

To return to the peace settlement with the Emperor and Shujauddowla. Lord Clive, who had lately returned to Bengal as the Company's Governor also came up to Allahabad. He signed a treaty with the Emperor, according to which the districts of Kora and Allahabad, worth about 48 lakh rupees a year, were given to the Emperor, together with an annual tribute of 26 lakhs. The rest of Oudh, with the exception of Benares and Gazipur, was restored to Nawab Shuja-ud-dowla, but he had to pay an indemnity of 50 lakh rupees to compensate for the Company's military expenses. After two copies of the treaty between the Nawab and the Company were drafted, signed and sealed, Lord Clive placed a Bible in the Nawab's hand, the Nawab put a Koran in Clive's hand, and the two embraced. Shortly afterwards Shuja-ud-dowla took leave of the Emperor and returned to his own domain. Through the treaty with the Emperor Clive obtained royal confirmation of the late Nawab Mir Zafar Ali Khan's son, Najim-ud-doula, as Nawab of Bengal, Bihar and Orissa, and for the Company the *diwani*, or revenue rights, to these regions in perpetuity. When Clive rose to take leave on signing the treaty, the Emperor addressed him with tears in his eyes: 'You have arranged the Company's affairs to your satisfaction,' he said, 'but you have done nothing to consolidate my position. You have not taken any step to station an English force that could help me rule from the throne of Delhi, and you now wish to abandon me amidst treacherous and treasonous people.'

Lord Clive and Colonel Carnac were distressed and somewhat ashamed to hear this. They replied: 'It is impossible to requisition an English Army without the express order of the King of England or the permission of the Company's directors. But now we will petition the King, stating all the facts, and as soon as the order arrives from England we will make haste to mobilise the army. Until then it is advisable that you should remain at Allahabad. Meanwhile, General Smyth, who commands part of the English Army, will be at your service with one battalion. Besides, an English Cantonment has been established near here in Jaunpur, and the entire force there will be able to assist you if necessary. Your Highness may therefore set your mind at rest. You may be assured that we are always ready to do your bidding.'

After this, in accordance with the Emperor's wishes two of his ministers, Nawab Muniruddowla and Raja Shitab Ray, prepared a draft of a letter to the English King, in which it was declared that an English army under England's command assigned to help administer the Indian Empire would be a symbol of friendship between the two kingdoms. It was also mentioned that the Indian Emperor had conferred the revenue rights of Bengal to the company as a token of goodwill to the English King and as a reward for services rendered by English troops. It was generally deemed fitting at the Court to send a present of one lakh rupees with the letter.

Nawab Muniruddoula and Raja Shitab Ray accompanied Lord Clive to Calcutta. Then, without the knowledge of the Company's Council of Members, they repaired with Colonel Carnac, Captain Swinton and the interpreter Mr. George Vansittart to the garden of Dumdum where after copying out the letter and impressing on it the royal seal of Badshah Shah Alam, they handed it in an embroidered cover to Captain Swinton, who was nominated to play the role of the Badshah's ambassador to the King of England. It was also felt necessary to send someone well-versed in Persian to represent the Badshah, and the choice fell unanimously on me. Nawab Muniruddoula gave me 4000 rupees to cover the expenses of the trip and held out hopes of the future favour of the Emperor. Youthful enthusiasm in conjunction with the pull of fate filled me with the desire to see Vilayet, and I embarked with Captain Swinton on the voyage.

After a week Captain Swinton told me that Lord Clive had taken Badshah Shah Alam's letter from him, saying that the present of one lakh had not arrived from Benares, without which it would not be proper to send the letter. Clive would himself come to England the following year, bringing both letter and present, which he would then entrust to Captain Swinton to take to the King. I was struck dumb by this information and clearly realised that a deep game was afoot, in which the journey was a mere pretext. Arduous and hazardous as it was, no advantage for me would ultimately accrue from it. If I had any inkling of this, I would not have undertaken it, but the matter was now out of my hands, the fateful step had been taken, the arrow had been shot from the bow and I could only watch helplessly as it sped along. So I helplessly surrendered to fate, and the will of Allah, and endured six months' hardship on the sea before we reached England. And in England I saw many rare and attractive things, but the joy in doing so was diminished by my constant preoccupation with the mystery of the missing letter, regarding which I quizzed Captain Swinton with exasperating frequency. I was in a pathetic situation in which I couldn't talk openly about what was weighing on my mind; nor did I have the courage or the means to do what I would have liked to with regard to it. My existence became a burden and I lived from day to day. For entertainment I tried to read books of history, but I felt no desire to master the English script. When on my return to Bengal my countrymen began chiding me for not having mastered the language of England during my long sojourn there, how could I reply without going into the entire mystery of the missing letter? Since I couldn't reveal anything about it I could only remain silent and pass for an ignoramus.

A brief account of the eastward explorations of the Firinghees

[Europeans] and their fortunes in India may not be out of place.

Historians tell us that just as the English are now more famous than all other nations, the Portuguese were once prominent among the Christian Kingdoms for their wealth and military might. Their ships were the first to reach Bengal and other parts of South Asia. Nearly two centuries ago, during Emperor Akbar's reign, they used to plunder the coasts of Malabar, Ceylon and Pegu; the pirates mentioned in contemporary chronicles as a menace to haj pilgrims were Portuguese.

Products from Bengal, like satin, muslin, silk and opium used to be in great demand in Europe, where they would fetch fantastic prices. This was due to the difficulties of transportation and the number of middlemen involved. Merchants took the goods in sloops and barges from the ports of Surat and Gujrat to Jedda and Basra and sold them to Arab traders, who in turn marketed them in Syria, Egypt and Turkey, where European traders procured them for their home markets. A bolt of satin that costs ten rupees in Bengal would in the end sell for fifty.

The Firinghees began thinking of searching out a sea route to the East so that their ships could trade directly with these regions. As this was before they invented the compass (which will be described in due course), when they did not possess the advanced shipbuilding and navigational skills they do now, they had to wait helplessly for want of sponsors. Finally, the Portuguese King, a bold and ambitious man, came forward. He fitted out a fleet of four or five ships, stocked it with food and other supplies sufficient to last a year, hired an efficient crew and well-trained officers, and bade them set sail.

The ships advanced slowly, covering no more than six to eight miles in a day. They continually took soundings and marked sandbanks and submerged rocks with warning signs for the benefit of those who would follow. The route closely followed the coastline, for without the compass it was impossible to navigate unfamiliar, open sea.

In one year the fleet covered about one hundred miles. They were nearly out of supplies, but it was easy to return quickly along the familiar course. The next year they set out again, and swiftly gaining the farthest point previously reached, began charting a course beyond it. Thus each year they charted a little more of the unknown. This laborious process caused the loss of several ships and many men.

Eventually the fleet reached a cape midway between Europe and India. It is a corner of the land of the *habshis*, or black people, and at the southern end of the world. The sailors reasoned that there couldn't be much of the earth left further to the south, and so by circumventing the cape they should be able to reach South Asia. For inspiring such optimism this point was named the Cape of Good Hope. When news of this discovery reached Europe the Firinghees threw their hats into the air for joy.

After nine years of struggle Portuguese ships reached India. They touched at Madras, Malabar, Ceylon and Pegu and returned home laden with the valuable products of these regions. The Firinghees were overjoyed at the success of the expedition, as if they had conquered the whole world. A second expedition came three years later, and another two years after it. Then they began coming every year. Firinghee scholars compiled guidebooks for the use of all Firinghee nations; these comprised sea-charts and maps indicating the salient features of South Asia. Before long all the hat-wearing nations of Europe – French, English, Dutch and Danish – came one after another and set up trading centres in Madras, Phoolchhari and Bengal. The wonderful and rare things they brought from Europe captivated the Indians.

During the reign of Badshah Akbar the Portuguese established control over Malabar, Ceylon and other islands, and began terrorising the coastal inhabitants, many of whom they kidnapped and sold into slavery. Consequently they were continually at odds with the imperial court. Akbar refused them permission to put up settlements, but under his successor, Jehangir, an embassy of Firinghees inveigled their way into royal favour by giving him many expensive presents from Europe. Jehangir allowed the Firinghees to build trading centres in the coastal areas in which they were living but forbade the construction of forts, moats and ramps for cannons. This prohibition was rigorously applied till the end of Aurengzebe's reign, and every royal edict to the Governor of Bengal adjoined particular watchfulness in this regard.

After Aurangzebe slackness and indiscipline became rife in the Mughal court, most notoriously during the recent reign of Muhammad Shah, who spent all his time in revelry and debauchery, without a thought for the responsibilities of administration. The princes became addicted to indolence and luxury. War trumpets gave way to tambourines and *tanpuras* [a stringed instrument]. The business of nautch- girls throve, and the racket they made disturbed the pious in their prayers. Paupers became emirs, while the true emirs hid themselves in the lap of decadence. Provincial governors managed the administration and finances just as they pleased and neglected the maintenance of armies, so that rebels and criminals became more and more daring in their depredations. The Portuguese and other Firinghees took advantage of the corruption and with presents of expensive European goods and large bribes, easily persuaded local officials to turn a blind eye while they built fortresses. The Portuguese built a fort in Balagarh, at the northern extremity of Hughli, where their church still stands. The English built their first fort in Bengal a little to the south of this, at Gholghat, where they still have an establishment. The Dutch fort at Chinsura and the Danish fort at Serampore still stand.

The expulsion of the Portuguese:
Together with the fort at Balagarh the Portuguese built a church, where they began worshipping idols of Christ, Mary and various Christian saints. The arrogance and lawlessness which mark their national character led them during Shaista Khan's governorship to flout the authority of the Mughal commandant and to get into unseemly fights. These would erupt whenever they went out to buy supplies, for they would try to bully the poor peasants and traders. They would also kidnap boys and girls and sell them into slavery in the islands off the Indian coast. During Sunday worship the clangour of their church bells rose to such a pitch that pious Muslims would be disturbed in their prayers or Koran-recitation. They ignored repeated requests of the Faujdar, or local Mughal Magistrate, to refrain from slave-trading and to ring their bells less noisily. Their arrogance rose to such heights that they prepared to attack the Faujdar. Even though they had only thirty European soldiers and one hundred and fifty Eurasian and native-Christian sepoys, they were bent on taking on the Mughals. Their fleet anchored in front of the Mughal fort at Hooghly and began a heavy bombardment. The Faujdar, the redoubtable Shukrullah, was at the house of the local Mansabdar, or Mughal governor. On hearing the very first shot he realised what was afoot and rushing into battle rode his horse into the water and

with mighty slashes of his sword severed the anchor-ropes of the Portuguese ships, thereby unsteadying the aim of their fire. Then he brought round his own ships to confront the Portuguese villains, who became totally unnerved and desperately sought escape. The Faujdar gave them hot chase. Aided by wind and current hunter and hunted sped south at full speed. When the fugitives reached Moghua, in front of the Muchilhola grove, they met with a fresh crisis. Following the Faujdar's orders, conveyed post-haste by riders, the local thanadar [the police officer-in-charge] had fixed heavy iron chains across the river. The Portuguese, however, broke through and made good their escape and took refuge in Ceylon, Malabar and other islands, where their earliest bases in the region were located.

Soon after this incident Allah visited a curse on the Portuguese in punishment of their villainous, tyrannical and piratical tendencies. A violent earthquake hit their capital and a massive tidal wave destroyed the royal palace. Only the affluent who could muster swift transport escaped with their lives; the poorer classes lost both life and property. Thus did the smile of good fortune vanish from Portugal. Its king became greatly reduced militarily and since then he hasn't tried to send any more expeditions to this country. The country is so small that if France, Russia, Spain or Germany wished they could easily annex it. But Allah had endowed the English with the greatest military might among all hat-wearing Firinghee nations and the English monarch has extended his protection to the Portuguese king.

The Expulsion of the English from Gholghat and the founding of Calcutta: When the English had their factory in Gholghat, not far from the Moghul fort at Hooghly, their unseemly conduct, such as the loud and frequent ringing of church bells, led to altercations with the Faujdar. Eventually Badshah Aurangzebe ordered them to move elsewhere. Mr. Charnock, then governor of the English factory, chose a village near Titgarh, which henceforth came to be known as Charnocknagar.

Since ancient times the English have been known for their ambition and doggedness, but now they became well-liked for their peaceful behaviour.

At this time Aurangzebe was preparing to round off his campaign in the South with an assault on the formidable Golconda fort, stronghold of the Shiite king of Hyderabad, Abul Hasan. A prolonged siege had depleted the Badshah's rations and material. On learning of this Mr. Charnock loaded all his ships with rations and rushed to the Mughal's assistance, arriving in time to save his army from starvation. Mr. Charnock was granted an audience at which he had the good fortune of being able to make obeisance to Aurangzebe and kissing the ground before his feet.

Mr. Charnock presented many rare objects from England to the Emperor. Subsequently he showed commendable zeal and initiative in helping with the digging of tunnels to undermine the foundations of the fort, thanks to which it was possible to take it in a short time. Mr. Charnock thus won his way into the Emperor's favour and when he requested for the East India Company the right to trade tax-free and the tax-free lease of forty bighas [bigha = approx. 1/3 acre] of land, the Emperor readily granted it. On his return to Bengal he established a factory on the newly obtained land; it became Calcutta.

Sobhan Allah! How ironical is fate! Those who only yesterday were supplicants for forty bighas of land are today masters of one half of India and have brought to their knees a host of proud and arrogant chieftains!

CHAPTER II

ON THE SEA AND SAILING

It was late January 1766. My preparations complete, I put my trust in Allah's mercy and got ready to board Monsieur Courville's ship at Higelee harbour. My friend Kazi Alimullah, who had come to see me off, took his leave. As the ship weighed anchor and spread sail, only Allah could have known the intensity of my grief at leaving my native land and kinsmen.

After four days' sailing down the Hooghly we reached the sea. Near the shore the water is a mixture of salinity and sweetness, and takes a whitish tint from the bed of the coastal shelf. Further away the sea becomes blue, and the foam of the waves gleams at night like lamps. Savants explain that the earth is girdled by a range of tall blue peaks known as the Caucasus. They lend their brilliant colour to the first firmament, which is otherwise clear as glass. The blue of the sea is a reflection of the sky. A simple proof of this is that sea-water scooped up with the hands appears whitish, if not colourless. As for the sea's salinity, it is due to the water's mixture with exhalations from the sea-bed. I had no choice but to use the salt water for bathing and ablutions.

Firinghee physicians believe that the sea air is beneficial for healthy and ailing alike. My experience bears them out. During my period at sea I was free from sickness save for a single case of stomach upset, which was readily cured with sherbet of *issop gool* [fleawort], prepared by soaking a pinch of fleawort seeds in a glass of water for a few hours.

An Account of the Vastness and the Unfathomable Depth of the Sea:
Let us not ever forget that complete knowledge of the secrets of the sea's depths belongs to Allah alone, and that we do not even

have an inkling about them. The little I have seen of the vastness and terrifying power of the sea testifies to Allah's infinite creative force.

The earth is like a floating egg amidst the sea's immensity. I have heard that in an attempt to plumb the sea's depth a Firinghee king had a rope dropped into it at the distance of a day's journey from the shore. Millions of yards disappeared and yet the rope didn't touch bottom. From this Firinghee scientists venture to conjecture that even if a shipload of rope no more in thickness than a man's little finger were dropped it wouldn't reach the sea-floor.

Indians who have no first hand knowledge of the sea believe that Alexander the Great plumbed and surveyed all the world's seas. It is an utterly erroneous belief. In no circumstances can it be true. The sea is bottomless; its furthest shores cannot be descried by the human eye. How then could Alexander or his scientists have fathomed its depths or measured its expanse? After all, they too were human.

But it is true, as we learn from Western histories, that the systematic measuring of land and sea distances began in Alexander's time. The unit of measure then used, the Alexandrine yard, is still known. Alexander measured the distance from Greece to Western Europe along the coast, for without the compass it was impossible to measure distances across the high sea. It is said that on his survey missions Alexander would advance slowly along the coast, taking careful measurements, and whenever a contrary wind forced him out to sea the Greek scientists, with great effort and care, would guide him back to shore. This was accounted a great scientific achievement.

European savants claim that Arabic and Persian historians have relied mainly on hearsay and incorporated contradictory accounts of the same incident. Consequently their writings have no more significance than fairy tales. This is notoriously true of their writings about Alexander, whom they make out as a paragon of virtue. They describe him as a model of justice, whereas in reality he was a tyrant. He practised no religion and went so far astray as to claim he was a god, yet he has been called a pious man, even a prophet. He was a characterless debauchee who has been described as a virtuous celibate.

But more authentic portraits of Alexander are also available, like the one written in Greek by one of his generals. Later Greek historians have opined that since Alexander was Greek the truth about him can be found only in the writings of other Greeks who knew him well. The Arab and Persian historians, writing from a great distance in space and time, could not but rely on hearsay. Surely there is a world of difference between what one hears and what one sees with one's own eyes.

The Compass:
Scientists believe that the metal, known as lodestone, from which the compass is made, was not known to Alexander or the scientists of the ancient world. It is only 200 years since scientists discovered it in the course of exploring the mountains of Arabia. Its innate property is to attract iron and it is used in making a compass in the following way. A line is drawn across the middle of a strip of this metal, dividing it into two parts, which are known as the head and the foot. The strip is then placed on a round vessel, and the midpoint of the dividing line is fixed on a sharp-pointed stone pivot so that it can revolve freely. A round card or metal disc affixed beneath the pivot is marked with the various directions – east, west, north, south, north-east, north-west, south-east, south-west – and further subdivisions are made to make a total of sixty-four points. The whole instrument is then suspended like a hot-air balloon. It now revolves at the slightest touch and when it settles again the metal needle points northward. Just as the Moslems determine direction with reference to the direction of Mecca, the hat-wearing Firinghees use the north for reference.

When a ship is far out to sea, alone with water and sky and no sign of lighthouse or shore, the Captain can navigate with the help of a compass and explore new routes, an account of which, together with maps and charts, is subsequently prepared in the form of a book, which anyone interested in navigation can study. This is how the Firinghees have made it safe for themselves to travel long distances. The compass is also used in determining distances across high seas. Truly the Europeans have attained astonishing mastery over the science of navigation.

The steersman controls a wheel which is connected to the rudder by a rope. If he rotates the wheel to right or left the rudder sympathetically responds and guides the ship in the desired direction. The Captain and his mates by turns station themselves near the steersman and with the help of the compass set a steady course. During storm or high wind at least two men are required to hold the wheel steadily. The Captain and his mates keep constant watch on the compass, take note of wind speed, and shout the necessary changes in direction from the compass, so that the steersman can hold the ship on course. In this manner the ship sails continuously, day and night, without anchoring. It makes port only to replenish its stores with fresh vegetables, water, chickens, lamb, etc.; to seek shelter from violent gales; or for repairs. Otherwise the Firinghees regard even an hour's delay as if it meant the loss of a month.

Throughout a voyage, frequent measurements of speed are taken in the following manner. One end of a rope long enough to circumscribe a four bigha plot [roughly an acre and a third] is fixed to one of the points of a triangular float about nine digits on each side. The rope is wound round a handled spool, which is held firmly by one sailor while another waits with hourglass in hand. At a signal the float is dropped into the sea and the hourglass simultaneously inverted. In calm sea the float remains still, with two of its points submerged and the third, to which the rope is attached, showing. There is a pull on the rope proportionate to the ship's speed, so it unreels steadily. But the very moment the sand runs out in the glass the unreeling of the rope is arrested. It is then hauled on board and the length that has unreeled read off to obtain the speed. This is now entered in a log-book, so that by looking up the many readings taken one can form a ready impression of the ship's average speed. The ship's speed, of course, varies considerably because of changes in the direction and speed of the wind. At the end of a day the Captain evaluates the ship's performance and enters the distance traversed that day into the log-book, together with the other details like the time spent at various ports, the daily temperature, difficulties encountered, accidents, etc.

Ships, their Varieties and Characteristics:
A single-masted vessel is a sloop, a two-masted one is a schooner, a three-master is a ship. The wooden masts are very tall and strong, and the strongest are those made of *sonali* wood. But the top and top-gallant masts, being rather narrow, are relatively vulnerable in a storm. At the approach of a storm sailors lower all sails except those on the lower masts, which are of *sonali*. Of course if a severe

storm catches a ship unawares at night the top and top-gallant masts are likely to snap. This happened to us on our return journey. The two lower masts, of *sonali*, remained intact, however, and with the help of these we continued sailing while the ship's carpenter and blacksmith fashioned a new pair of masts to replace the broken ones.

A broken mast slows down a ship, but there is otherwise no danger. The ships are designed to withstand violent gales, unlike our country boats, which are liable to turn turtle in heavy weather. Their hulls are shaped like the rib-cages of birds – an efficient design introduced when Noah built his ark on Gabriel's instructions.

The masts are firmly held in place by ropes and the sails, which are of various sizes, are likewise fastened securely with ropes fixed to huge nails driven into the deck. Each sail and each rope has a specific name. Since the sails have to be arranged in accordance with the direction and speed of the wind – sometimes facing full front, sometimes spread obliquely, at times furled or lowered – the Captain and his mates take turns watching over them and should any rearrangements become necessary, call out the names of the relevant ropes and sails and order the required changes, which the sailors can make readily, using pulleys.

A ship generally has five storeys. The topmost storey is aft and is occupied by the Captain and his officers; all valuables are stored in the saloon there. The storey immediately below is divided into three sections. The foremost one houses the kitchen and galley, the middle is taken up by sailors' quarters, where they sleep in hammocks slung from the roof, and aft are the cabins of paying passengers. Both sides of this storey also have gun emplacements. The next two storeys are for the storage of food and provisions, and for cargo, and the lowest storey is where sand is carried as ballast. As ships tend to attract vapours from the sea, the bilge contains much water, which needs to be bailed out continuously. As a precaution against leakage the joints in the wood are reinforced with jute and straw. This is sufficient to resist the pressure of the water outside, unless the ship runs into a sand bank or a rock.

During high wind the waves slap against the hull with resounding cracks and the entire ship trembles as if there was an earthquake. Those without experience of the sea are liable to be driven to panic and to be seized with fear of imminent shipwreck, as I can tell from my own experience. I was however soon reassured, as I learned more about the nature of these ships, that all was well. The waves can rise as high as palm trees; but if the ship lists, such is its design, that it is at once righted by the pressure of the waves from the sides. In choppy sea the portholes and doors are all kept tightly shut, and the waves may wash over the top deck without endangering the vessel.

Description of Various Winds:
If the wind blows squarely from behind it fills the rearmost sails first and is a spent force by the time it reaches the sails in front. In such an event the sailors lower the rear sails, for the wind blowing into them makes the ship sway and dip in such a way as to induce seasickness in passengers. It is best when the wind blows from the side, whether port or starboard; it makes for smooth and speedy sailing. However, the windward side is tilted upward, and the leeward side is not more than two cubits above the water. When I first saw this happen I was fearful that the ship would sink immediately, but Captain Swinton reassured me saying, 'It is not one of your Indian ships, that it will sink so easily.'

A contrary wind of moderate speed can do no more than slow down a ship. If a convoy sails into the wind in single file, only the leading ship suffers loss of speed. This was borne upon me during a spell of contrary wind when I saw that the seventy ships following us in convoy in a straight line had no difficulty in maintaining speed, while ours had to struggle.

A violent contrary wind can drive a ship hundreds or even thousands of miles and also damage it considerably. May Allah protect all ships from such a fate! A gale blowing from the side can also drive a ship off course. The heavy clouds and fogs that accompany the storm obliterate the distinction between day and night and a ship incurs the risk of running into submerged rocks or sandbanks and breaking apart from the impact. When the storm subsides it is possible to get back on course with the help of a compass. But if the storm rages too long and the ship loses its masts and runs out of food and fresh water it becomes much more difficult for it to do so. Then it is heaven-sent to chance upon an isle or coastal village where supplies can be replenished and repairs made, after which it is possible to resume the journey with a light heart. If, however, the storm-tossed ship is carried so far away that it cannot make land quickly, and if its provisions are exhausted, certain death is the lot of those on board.

A ship running into a submerged rock is instantly wrecked and disappears without a trace. There are many tales of such disasters. Recently, when after defeating Nawab Sirajuddowla at Plassey, the English started building a fort in Calcutta, a newly commissioned ship of the East India Company carrying men and material for the Government's defence, including one hundred and fifty large cannons, five hundred White troops, a Captain and several officers, was wrecked in this manner. As it made for Madras after rounding the Cape, a violent storm drove it into a sandbank that stood barely two cubits above the water. The ship disintegrated on impact. Sixty of the men reached the safety of the shore, either by swimming or with the help of floating debris. The rest perished. The ship's cargo included chests of munitions, goods for trade, bales of cloth, sackloads or rice and flour, bread and biscuits from England, and casks of water and wine. Some of this, as also wooden planks from the wreck, were washed ashore and seized by the survivors as heaven-sent. One of them was a gentlewoman. No sooner had she dried herself in the sun when the body of her drowned husband was washed ashore. On seeing it she let out an anguished shriek and gave up her ghost. The shipwreck was caused by a hill whose tip stood barely a yard above water, but whose base area was at least forty square miles. The coast where the survivors landed was bare of trees or any other vegetation, but there were wild fowl, which they hunted for food. They toiled with great determination and in sixteen days built a boat and reached Madras. There are many such stories of shipwrecks.

Not only are Europeans very able navigators, but they endeavour continuously to increase their competency. The new skills and knowledge they acquire are simplified and systematised, so that they may be easily taught to novices. This they do not only in the case of navigational science but of other branches of learning as well. This trait is peculiar to Europeans. Their courage and industry have made them the most powerful race on earth.

The rigours and dangers they willingly bear are beyond the endurance of any other people. During a storm, if the sails need to be rearranged or taken down, they will climb to the top and top-gallant masts with the agility of Hanuman and hang from there like bats. They haven't the least fear in their hearts, as I can testify. One stormy night the three top-gallant masts were carried away and a Firinghee sailor on a top-gallant yard fell overboard with it. One of the ship's watches, who was standing near the gangway, threw him a rope and called out to him to catch hold of it. The man wound the rope round his hand and was hauled on board, uninjured. Within an hour he was back at work, as if nothing had happened.

When a storm blows over it gives way to a gentle and very pleasant breeze that slows down the ship and brings solace to the storm-tormented passengers. However, the sooner the ship can resume its normal progress, the better it is for the passengers. Sometimes it may happen that there is no breeze at all. The ship lies becalmed, masts swinging lazily from side to side. The sea is a clear blue mirror extending on all sides to the horizon. These calm spells last at least a week or two. Our ship was held up once in this manner. The sailors gave themselves up to singing and merriment and the gentlemen passengers enjoyed themselves by dancing with the ladies. All this appeared very strange to me. I was filled with the dread thought that if the ship remained there much longer we would all starve to death and I would be deprived of the good fortune of ever seeing my native land again.

CHAPTER III

MAURITIUS AND OTHER PLACES

It was late March when we arrived in Mauritius. There I met a Sareng [an officer of the lascars] from Chittagong and seven other Moslem lascars from Hooghly, Vellore and Shahpur. They had come to the port city to pray at the Eid congregation that marks the end of Ramadan. They had all settled on the island and had no inclination to return to their own country, having, so to speak, married into slavery. Their wives were slaves of French masters who wouldn't in any case allow them to leave the island. I was glad to meet my countrymen, whose hospitality ensured my comfort during the sixteen days we stayed there. But I also grieved inwardly because they had forsaken their own land.

Mauritius has a perimeter of 600 miles. The central part is taken up by hills, woods and wild tracts, but the eastern coast has two to three thousand bighas of cultivated land and a small city where the French have built a factory and a fort.

The French notables live in mansions built on stockaded plots of a couple of bighas in the middle of their estates, which are cultivated with the help of a hundred or so male and female slaves. Oranges, Indian corn and vegetables are grown for the market. One half of the proceeds goes to the landlord, the other half is divided among the slaves. These slaves are brought as adolescents from Bengal, Malabar, the Deccan and other regions and sold for fifty to sixty rupees each.

The wealthy Mauritians eat fine wheat and rice imported from Bengal, Malabar or Europe, and the poor natives live on Indian corn, the only grain produced on the island. They also pound a radish-like root plant into flour and bake bread with it. I found it utterly insipid – neither sweet nor sour not salty nor bitter.

With the help of my lascar acquaintances, who acted as my interpreters, I purchased mangoes, water-melons, cucumbers, musk-melons and several other varieties of fruits peculiar to the Bengali summer. The mangoes weighed from half to one pound, were free of fibres and had an excellent flavour. There was one species of mango rarely seen in Bengal, green on the outside, blue inside, firm of flesh and sweet to taste. The small thin-skinned lime, *kagazi nimboo*, and the red chilli grow wild in the hills and are picked by the poor and sold in the bazaar.

Copper coins and cowries are not used in Mauritius, but there is a paper currency in denominations ranging from one to one hundred rupees, which is the sole medium of exchange.

The air is humid, rainfall heavy, and soil sandy; consequently mud houses are impractical. Houses here are entirely of wood, and built on stilts one or two cubits high. The walls are of wooden planks and the roofs, grass or straw being rare, are made of planks overlapping like tiles and are fixed in place with iron nails. Not a drop of rainwater can get through. These houses will stand without any repairs for fifty to a hundred years. As they are on stilts they can be easily put on wheels and transported to another site.

Mauritius is difficult of access. Coastal hills deny landing to ships except in the east where the island's only harbour is situated. Even this had to be approached by a six-mile long channel, which is quite hazardous. Those unfamiliar with its course may find it well nigh impossible to negotiate. So it is hardly surprising that it is the only French island in this region that the British failed to take during the recent war between the two countries. An English force under Captain Weatherburn launched a number of attacks on it, without success.

It is reported that the Portuguese were the island's first colonisers, but they found it so heavily infested with snakes, serpents, scorpions and other noxious creatures that they were soon forced to abandon it. After them the French moved in and had better luck. French priests using a kind of necromancy caught the dangerous creatures, took them out to sea and drowned them. Since then there is no sign of them on the island. Of course Allah alone knows how far the story is true.

Fish abound in the waters around the island and are caught by the islanders with hook, spear and net. A few species resemble Bengali fish, though they aren't exactly the same. One is like the anabas, but with a wider mouth; another resembled our *puti*. It too had a wide mouth. It was also attractively coloured (white, with red spots) and was excellent to taste. Other fish resembled the *kholisa* and the *boal* and these too were quite good to eat.

The day after we landed in Mauritius a violent cyclone struck. For three days the wind raged and rain fell in torrents. Two heavily laden French merchantmen dragged anchor and were wrecked on the treacherous rocks to the east of the harbour. Our ship was also driven in that direction and was run foul of by a Spanish man-of-war. We suffered serious damage but thanks to Allah's mercy and the efforts of our sailors we returned safely to our anchorage. One of our outer planks broke, causing a huge leak and a couple of telescopes mounted on the top deck were smashed. This necessitated time-consuming repairs, which is why we had to spend so many days there.

Among the vessels wrecked in this storm was a French ship that had started with us from Higely; it was caught in the storm before it could reach Mauritius and was swept far and wrecked. Later, when we neared the Cape, we saw its wreckage. If the storm had caught us in the high sea, our fate would have been the same. We thanked Allah for saving us from such an end. Mercifully there were no more storms of such severity, nor any other misfortune, till we reached Europe.

One day Captain Swinton and Mr. Peacock, another passenger, said to me jokingly, 'It is owing to the presence of your prosperous foot that we have survived the danger.' They were referring to the belief in lucky feet, which like the belief in the evil eye, is prevalent among Moslem and Hindu Indians alike.

I replied, 'I am an impure creature from whom no advantage will come. It is owing to the mercy of Allah the Preserver that his servants aboard this ship are safe and can hope to see green fields once again.'

On our way to Mauritius we had passed by many interesting islands and coasts on the Indian Ocean. To the south-east of Bengal there is a Portuguese island called Batavia, whose inhabitants included Moslems, Dutchmen, Englishmen and dark-complexioned natives, besides Portuguese colonists. Chillies, pepper, cinnamon, cardamom and other spices grow in abundance here, as also do varieties of fruits. Further in the same direction, about two months' journey from Bengal, is an island, which is a part of the Chinese kingdom and is famous for its Chinaware.

Pegu and Malacca:
These are populous countries lying to the south-east of Bengal at a distance of half a month's voyage. Tahir Mohammed, an emir at the court of Badshah Akbar, during a long stint as ambassador to the court of Adil Shah, Sultan of Bejapur in the Deccan, wrote a book called the *Rowza-t-ut-fahereen* ['*Garden of the Immaculate*'], where there are accounts of all the countries in the region, including Pegu.

According to Tahir, in former times the people of Pegu had no religion and were ignorant of the distinction between right and wrong, the lawful and the forbidden. Among them went a Sayyid – a descendant of the Prophet Mohammed – from Bengal. He introduced these people to Islam in the following manner. He was in the habit of reciting loudly and mellifluously from the Koran. The natives were charmed by the recitation and began gathering regularly to listen to him. Gradually they began emulating his religious practices – praying, fasting, giving the azan or call to prayer – and were soon received into Islam. At the request of native leaders the Sayyid became their Imam and King, that is, both their religious and secular Chief. To this day his descendants are the nobles among the population of Pegu, who still follow Islam.

Tahir narrates an extraordinary tale, well-known in Bengal, about this Sayyid. He is said to have captured a fairy, who lived with him for seven years and bore him children. But at last the fairy's true nature triumphed. She became faithless and deserting husband and children, returned to her native realm.

Mangoes, coconuts, watermelons, cucumbers and varieties of rice grow in abundance in Pegu, and its forested hills yield valuable teakwood and abound with deer, wild horses, donkeys, goats and sheep.

Malacca is nearly as large as Bengal. Its interior is inhabited by aborigines who are dark as habshis and of robust health. They have satanical countenances and bestial natures. They do not care for any religion and lack all moral sense. They are always on the lookout for plunder among the peasants of Malacca, who live along the coast. The two peoples are therefore in a state of continuous war. The Mallaccan peasants grow grain of all kinds, bananas and mangoes, but the diet of the aborigines is usually raw or half-dressed meat; their dress is untanned animal hides. Tahir's book mentions some barbarous practices among them. If one of them is laid up with fever, a joyful meeting of his neighbours is convened to plan his end. They kill the patient without any hesitation and make kebabs with his flesh, which they then devour with relish. It is also common among them to wager their own flesh from the thighs and posterior. The winner cuts off the wagered quantity – which may be as much as two pounds – and makes a feast of it. The loser mashes the leaves of a certain medicinal plant and applies them to the wound. It takes ten to twelve days to heal and leaves no cicatrix, and the loser can move about as effortlessly and rapidly as he used to.

As we sailed down the Bay of Bengal, Malacca showed as a thin black line on the horizon.

South-west of Madras, at a distance of one-hundred miles – or a day's sailing – from Pondicherry, lies Ceylon, which Indians call Serendip. The footprint of Adam lies preserved on this island, which is about one hundred and fifty miles across and abounds with sapphires and other precious stones.

The Maldives:

This group of islands is situated to the south of Madras. Its sovereign is inferior in power and wealth to a zemindar [feudal landlord] of Bengal, yet he affects the title of Badshah. The inhabitants are Moslem, but have little knowledge of the articles of religion. The soil is sandy and consequently there is little agriculture. But coconut trees are innumerable, and provide the islanders' livelihood. The kernel of the coconut is eaten and coconut oil is used for cooking and in lamps. The houses are built of the timber and leaves of the coconut tree. Coir is spun into ropes, which are tempered by soaking in coconut oil. These ropes are exported as far as Europe and are used in securing ships' anchors. All the coconut oil imported into Bengal comes from the Maldives.

Maldiveans build large boats with planks from coconut trees. No iron nails are used, but coir ropes bind the planks together. The boats are so strong that they can even withstand storms on high sea. Maldivean traders bring boatloads of coconuts to the markets of Madras and Balasore and return with cloth, rice, sugar, etc.

I have heard that the Maldives include several thousand small islands, the waters around which abound with cowries. These are collected in the following manner. The Badshah of the Maldives owns a large fleet of five hundred to a thousand boats. During low tide these sail to unfrequented spots and dig holes. At high tide the sea fills the holes with cowries. When the tide recedes the cowries are left behind in the holes. The boatmen load them into their boats and take them away. The collected cowries are left in a ditch, where they soon die, and their flesh rots away. When the insides of the shells dry up they are gathered in heaps and sold to merchants from Bengal and other places.

The Island of the Cannibals [Madagascar?]:
The inhabitants of this island are human, yet their physiognomy is diabolical. They dress in the skins of wild beasts and eat half-raw meat. They crave human flesh, and, there being gold mines on the island, they will gladly barter gold for men. When they espy a vessel in the distance, they light a fire on a hill in order to lure the ship to their shores. Those unaware of the nature of the islanders imagine the beacon to be a friendly invitation and cast anchor near the shore so that they may rest a little and replenish their stores with provisions. The satanical natives gather in troops and by deceit and stratagem plunder and murder the ship's crew and consider the ship their lawful prize. If a vessel is wrecked and cast upon their shores it is dealt with in the same manner. There is a well-known story of a certain Mr. Henry, whose ship was wrecked on this island on its way to Europe. The islanders devoured the entire crew and it was by a miracle that Mr. Henry escaped their attentions and managed to find his way back to civilisation. Another vessel, sent to survey the island, was also seized and those on board devoured. Since then ships try to avoid the island. If it is forced to stop there for provisions it anchors at a safe distance and sends heavily armed boatloads of crewmen to obtain the necessities. If they wish to procure gold, they take a murderer or a thief, who is proper subject for slaughter, and barter him for the precious metal.

CHAPTER IV

ROUNDING THE CAPE

After Mauritius our course lay south-west. When, after a month's journey, we reached the equator, the heat became intolerable. Captain Swinton showed me a map of the world and said, 'Here, directly to the north, lie Arabia and the city of Mecca.'

As we neared the Cape we ran into a violent contrary wind that blew without let for twenty-six days and forced us back about a thousand miles. I learned that such winds are a common feature of this region, and make navigation an arduous task. When the wind abated a little we rounded the Cape with great difficulty and set a course to the north-west.

On my return journey from Vilayet our ship anchored at Cape Town for a fortnight, during which I gathered some information about the place. The Cape is a promontory of the land of the *habshis* and is the southernmost tip of the earth. There is no human settlement for about one thousand, five hundred miles to the north, only mountains and forests. This wild region is bounded on the north by a mighty river, about six miles wide, running to the sea from the mountains in the *habshi* country to the west. In summer it is only a knee-deep trickle bounded by sand flats. Across the river is *habshi* country and beyond that the land of the cannibals, where there are many gold mines. Trading ships go there and obtain gold in exchange for guns and gew-gaws, which the savages are very fond of. Further beyond lies the land of the fuzzy-haired, thick-lipped kaffirs.

One of the habshi kingdoms, Abyssinia, is near Arabia. Its king bears the title of Negus. One of its former kings had the honour of embracing Islam during the prophet's lifetime. The inhabitants of the country are black or brown complexioned. There is an age-old conflict between infidel kaffirs and Moslems, who have made it their practice to sell kaffir prisoners of war to slavers, who in turn sell them in far-flung lands.

When the hat-wearing Firinghees appeared in the region they tried to establish colonies for their respective nations. The Cape came under the dominion of the Dutch, who have built a beautiful city, Cape Town, on the sea and planted different varieties of European and Indian trees, such as the vine, apple, pear, quince and plantain. The citizens are enthusiastic horticulturists and plant cypress and box trees in their gardens.

Before the Dutch settled in the Cape it was a wilderness, and the dark-skinned nomadic forest-dwellers were the only people who might be seen. They would come from outside the Cape in groups sometimes numbering as much as seven to eight thousand, with their horses, sheep and cattle, and would settle in one place for three or four years before moving on. Their clothing is undressed skins, their diet raw and half-cooked meat, milk, and wild fruits. They are well-built and of a good stature, and are so swift and agile in the chase that they can catch wild boars and deer with ease. They are also expert at obtaining the precious ivory from the huge elephants of the region. They dig deep pits in the elephants' haunts, and when the elephant herds come from the hills and jungles to graze, they make a loud din and drive them towards the pits, into which they fall in a heap. They let the animals die of starvation and rid them of their tusks, which they sell to ivory merchants.

These nomadic people stopped coming to the Cape when it became a Dutch colony, and those of them who were here at the time wandered off, never to return. The Dutch buy men, women and children in Bengal and bring them to the Cape. I met some of these slaves. They had almost no Bengali or Hindustani, but using sign language I was able to obtain the information given above. They caught fish for me and also brought me fruits like mangoes and guavas.

After a month's voyage in a north-westerly direction from the Cape we reached the uninhabited island of Ascension. Most of it is rocky, with only a single pool of water at the centre, formed by rain water, from where sailors obtain fresh water. The rocks around the pool have a curious burnt or half-burnt appearance, like the porous overburnt bricks, called *jhama* in India.

Fish are plentiful. There was a species resembling the crow-fish: the head is large, the mouth gaping, the body covered with black scales. They are of excellent flavour and were caught in large numbers by the sailors, who used hooks for the purpose.

The island has huge sea turtles, each weighing as much as two to three maunds [1 maund – approx. 82 lbs.]. On moonlit nights, when they climbed onto the sandy beach to lay eggs the ship's Firinghee sailors concealed themselves and lay in wait. At an opportune moment they would rush forward, seize a turtle and overturn it. Forty to fifty were caught in one night. The eggs and flesh of the turtle were a great treat to the crew. One turtle was sufficient to provide a day's meat for the whole ship.

There are many varieties of waterfowl and numerous birds whose flesh may be eaten. As there are neither trees nor grass on the island, the birds don't build nests, but live in pairs in the shelters of hills and rocks. It seemed to me that in the past they either lacked acquaintance with man or didn't suffer at their hands; consequently they would, presumably, regard man as a harmless species of animal and go up to him fearlessly. With increase in shipping they of course see more of man, but they haven't yet learned the art of survival in the face of human predatoriness, for when sailors tried to seize them, instead of fleeing for their lives they merely shrieked and pecked ineffectually at the hands of the attackers. Eleven birds were captured. The men gave me two, which I took on board and handed over to my servant Muhammad Mukeem, who slaughtered them according to Islamic rites, cleaned them and cooked them ghee with hot spices. But the meat wouldn't become tender or lose an unpleasant odour. At last we threw the whole dish into the sea. The Firinghees, however, ate the bird with relish, having grilled them on a fire. Firinghees, particularly the French, are really very dirty eaters. The French Firinghees on the ship were unspeakable in their ways.

Because of the scant grass there are no quadrupeds on the island with the exception of a few sheep, offspring of a ram and an ewe left there by a French Captain. He also put into a bottle a slip of paper with a request that the sheep should not be molested. To ensure that visiting ships didn't miss the bottle he placed it on an eminence and planted a flagstaff beside it.

Before reaching Ascension we had passed the British island of St. Helena on our left. It has a commanding mountain with a town and a citadel atop, which however, we were too far to see clearly. After leaving Ascension we passed several more islands of varying sizes which belong to Portugal. Gigantic tongues of flame rose from one of these. I was told that this inferno raged day and night. Some said it indicated the presence of gold underground, others called it the handiwork of Satan. Allah alone knows the truth.

Far to our west, beyond the reach of human sight lay the coast of the huge continent the Firinghees call the Western Hemisphere. It comprises many islands, large and small, and its area is more than two or three times that of India. It is considered a part of the Firinghee world, though it is not included among the seven geographical regions of the world. The natives of this continent are dark-skinned, illiterate and stupid. They are ignorant of religion, statecraft and the art of war. As a result every hat-wearing Firinghee nation has been able to establish colonies there. White-skinned Firinghees have settled there in large numbers and there is brisk traffic of European trading ships to and from the colonies.

The ocean is full of wonders. If I described them all my book would become too bulky, so let me just give a few short notes.

The Flying Fish:

In appearance it resembles the *dewa* fish of India. It is about ten inches long. It has a pair of wings about five to six inches long, subtler than a spider's web and of a finer texture than silk paper. Flying fish become greatly agitated at the approach of a ship and flocks of them begin to fly alongside it at a height of thirty feet or so above the water. They can fly only as long as their wings are moist. As soon as they become dry from the action of the sun and wind, they drop into the water, and sometimes on the ship's deck. The sailors then promptly catch them and dress them by placing a pinch of opium in their bellies, which acts as a preservative. They are later sold at fantastic prices in India, where doctors consider them a powerful stimulant and prescribe them as a cure for impotence.

The Whale:
It is at least equal in bulk to two full-grown elephants; often it is larger. Its neck resembles an elephant's, and its nose too is rather like an elephant's trunk, only much smaller. Its nostrils are on the crown of its head. Each time it inhales, water gets into its throat and when it exhales this water is expelled like a fountain as tall as a date palm and so noisy that it can be heard a mile away.

Whether out of curiosity or in the hope of getting food, several whales approached our ship and swam around it, sometimes on the surface, sometimes just beneath. If, while rising to the surface, one of them had struck the ship, even lightly, she might have been bilged. It's an alarming thought; each time a whale approached I felt a twinge of panic.

The Sea Cow:
Savants estimate that Allah has created four thousand different species that dwell on the earth's surface, in air, or in water. Among them are many strange creatures, like the djinn, whose substance is fire, and who can assume any shape at will, and the sea cow that comes on land at night to deposit its ambergris-sweet excrement. Some say that this is the authentic ambergris. The ambergris-dung dries into cakes that float in the tide. Sailors can collect them without landing, and sell them in the market at a high price. Brahmins and other Hindus well versed in the Vedas call the sea cow the cow of Kailash, i.e. a heavenly cow, Kailash being the mountain abode of Siva. They say that sea cows fly to earth from Mt. Kailash for brief visits.

The Hog Fish:
It is really a species of seal. It owes its name to the fact that its head resembles that of a hog. It is black in colour, has no scales on its body, and weighs about two maunds. When it senses the presence of a ship from a distance it approaches joyfully and leaps like wild deer around it. Like a groom chasing an errant horse it follows the ship for eighty to one-hundred miles. At least a thousand hog-fish sported in this manner around our ship. When they leapt all together there was a noise like a tempest. It was an entertaining spectacle.

A firinghee sailor shot one of these fish and succeeded in landing it on board. It was grilled and served at table, but the flesh was so foul-smelling that I could hardly eat a morsel. European physicians hold that the flesh of very large fish is unwholesome, but the Europeans on our ship suffered no harm from eating the hog-fish.

The Mermaid:
The mermaid is a beautiful woman from head to waist, with a shapely pair of breasts, a mouth like a flower, black tresses, dark eyes, eyebrows curved like a bow. On seeing her even the most unromantic man feels an anguished agitation in his heart, and passionate youths are driven moon-mad with love. Her lower half, however, is like that of a fish with a forked tail. A mermaid's effigy is often placed on the sterns and stems of ships.

There are no mermaids in India, but sailors are reported to have sighted them in adjoining seas. Their appearance, which usually occurs in dangerous waters, is considered a bad omen. May Allah in his infinite mercy prevent anyone from seeing a mermaid, for it is a kind of genii. When a mermaid sits upright in the water, revealing the whole of her lovely torso, the sailors are bewitched at the sight. She then calls one of them by name in a high-pitched voice. The person addressed immediately grows restive and when the call is repeated, prepares to leave ship. At the third summons he leaps into the water and is never seen or heard of again. It is said that nothing can hold him back from answering the third call, not even iron chains. The mermaid conveys her chosen victim to a deserted island, tends him carefully, feeds him on fruits and cohabits with him.

According to an old story a ship in distress once put in at a remote island and there found a man who had been carried off by a mermaid and later forsaken. The experience had wrought such a change in him that he had become mute. The ship's crew took him on board, but failed to restore his power of speech, and so the particulars of his extraordinary experience remain unknown. Allah alone knows the truth of this story.

CHAPTER V

VILAYET AT LAST

Our ship anchored a couple of miles from the shore at the French port of Nantes. One of our guns fired a signal, in response to which a pilot boat was sent to guide us to the wharf of the French East India Company. The whole operation took about two hours.

As soon as we docked vendors flocked to the ship bearing fruits, bread, cheese, biscuits and butter. The sailors, who had not seen such fresh fare for six months, regaled themselves on it, and were generally overjoyed at seeing their homeland again. I could well understand their feelings. For six months I too had seen hardly anything besides sea and sky, and like a caged bird I was continually counting the ship's planks to pass time and to keep at bay the terrifying thought that the ocean might have no end. The sight of dry land and human habitation infused new life into my frame.

One thing astonished me. The lower orders among the French are so poor that they cannot afford shoes, and as a substitute wear wooden sandals. They take small blocks of wood and chiselling holes of the appropriate size they slip their feet into them and walk about with a ludicrous shuffle.

There are poor people in England too, but they do not suffer for want of leather boots and socks. Captain Swinton and Mr. Peacock laughed at the sight of the miserable Frenchmen in their comical footwear and said, 'These people are so wretched because they are not industrious like the English. They are very indolent.'

Since an edict of the French king forbids private citizens to import merchandise from the East, Customs officials came on board and stationed guards to make sure that passengers' baggage didn't get mixed up with the Company's cargo. If anyone is caught trying to smuggle in goods, these are confiscated and a penalty imposed. The

Captain's mates, a doctor, and a priest, who brought pieces of cotton cloth from Bengal concealed them in their pockets and on their person, tying them round their waists and chests, put on their usual clothes on top, and stole past the guards like thieves. Captain Swinton and Mr. Peacock went to look for lodgings in the town. I had to remain on board for two or three days more, during which time I learned a little about the people of the region and their laws and customs.

Man steals from his own pocket, runs a proverb. I found ready proof of its truth in the behaviour of Captain Swinton and Mr. Peacock. They had brought gold, silver, varieties of cloths and other valuable goods, which they had no difficulty in taking off the ship as the French officials were lenient towards Englishmen. They then entrusted the goods with transporters on the understanding that they would smuggle them into England concealed in consignments of fruits and vegetables.

After sixteen days in Nantes I parted company with Captain Swinton and Mr. Peacock. They set off for England in a fast post-chaise, while I set sail in a sloop. A week later I reached Calais, where I spent two weeks as a house guest of the sloop's Captain. I spent my time in walking about the streets and markets, observing the architecture and way of life of the townspeople, as well as the agricultural practices in the surrounding countryside. Wheat, maize, mustard, lentils, peas, radishes, watermelons, spinach, oranges, grapes, guavas, pears, apples and pomegranates grow much better here than in England. The latter, being further to the north, is subject to severe cold weather and snowfall, which do not conduce to the growth of fruits and vegetables. However, even in France fruits peculiar to the Arab world, like pistachio, and fruits and crops peculiar to India, like rice, *mash kalai* [a kind of pulse], mangoes, coconuts, bananas, aubergines, etc. cannot be seen at all.

The houses in the country are built of stone slabs, with roofs of terra cotta tiles. As the bamboo doesn't grow here the scaffolding for the roofs is built of wood. The poorer classes live on a diet of broth and barley-bread and wear coarse wool or clothes woven from hemp, of which ropes are also spun. Most of them cannot afford leather shoes.

Paris, the capital of France, is several hundred miles from either Calais or Nantes. Frenchman and foreigner alike sing high praises of the buildings and gardens of that city, its artistic innovativeness, scientific and technological advancement, the polished manners, cultivation, well-spokenness and wit of its inhabitants. In these respects it far surpasses all other cities in the Firinghee world.

The French claim that they have taught music and horsemanship to the English. Wealthy Englishmen send their children to French schools to polish up their manners and taste. The French say that the present excellence of the English in the arts and sciences, trade and industry, is the result of French education; in the past, when they lacked this education, they were ignorant like the mass of Indians. However, even the French admit that the English have always been outstanding soldiers.

The French say that the lower classes of Englishmen do not go to foreign countries to seek trade or employment because, being stupid and without any skills or business acumen, they would fail to earn a decent livelihood. The French, on the other hand, are skilled in all the arts and sciences, and wherever they go they are cordially received and acquire dignity and honour in diverse professions.

I realised clearly that the French are a conceited race, whose conversation was always an attempt to display their own superiority and to unfairly belittle other nations.

It also became clear to me that knowledge and skill in the arts are a great gift from Allah and anyone who wilfully neglects to acquire them is a stupid wretch. Such, alas, is my fate! My life so far has gone by aimlessly, and so will what remains of it.

From Calais I took a packet boat going to England. It took us a day to reach the small English port of Dover. Customs officials came on board to inspect our luggage and in the trunk of Mrs. Peacock, who was of mixed Portuguese and Indian parentage, they discovered a roll of flowered cotton and another of kincob. As it was a punishable offence to bring these items into the country the boat was seized with everything on board and taken up a narrow canal that came down to the sea. The mouth of the canal was then closed by securing a heavy wooden gate. I disembarked, put up at an inn, and after despatching a letter to Captain Swinton in London, in which I gave an account of all that had transpired, I occupied myself in sightseeing through the streets and bazaars of the town and its environs.

The English had never seen an Indian dressed as I was. They considered me a great curiosity and flocked to have a look. As I was a foreigner they showed me great kindness and hospitality and after a few days treated me as an old acquaintance. The friendliness of the English and, more particularly, the sight of their lovely women dispelled the sorrow of solitude and cheered me greatly.

One day some people took me to a dance party at the house of one of their friends. As soon as I entered, the music and dancing stopped. The assembled ladies and gentlemen thronged round me in wide-eyed amazement and examined my robe, turban, shawl and other parts of my costume. They concluded that it was the costume of a dancer or actor and invited me to joint the dance. I protested that I had no knowledge of the art of dancing, but they refused to believe me. They said there was nobody on earth who didn't know something of music and dancing. One of the English gentlemen said that as I was newly arrived in England I was perhaps feeling shy to dance with ladies of another race. At this the ladies tittered with amusement. They continued to stare at my clothes and countenance, while I gazed at their astonishing loveliness. How ironic that I, who had gone there to enjoy a spectacle, became a spectacle myself. In such attractive company, I mused, even the wisest are apt to lose their wits. The ladies were lovely as houris; their beauty would have shamed even fairies into covering their pretty faces. I could not distinguish between the brightness of the lamps and the splendour of their appearance. Speechless with admiration, I stood like a statue, and overwhelmed by the glory of Allah's creative power, recited this distich to myself:

> Out of dust he produces a living body,
> And from seed makes a fair face.

Not long after, Captain Swinton and Mr. Peacock came down from London with release orders for our belongings. The packet boat was freed from custody and sent on to London, whither we now travelled by coach. There Captain Swinton took me to his brother's house in Coventry Street, near Haymarket.

Just as I had been depressed by the hardships of the voyage, I now felt elated by the beautiful sights of London town, amidst which my homely face was like a leafless plant in a flowering rose garden. But though I was far from being well-dressed, the English were pleased to receive me, and treated me kindly. It is a sign of the generosity of the English, which I cannot find words to describe or praise. A traveller from abroad is dearer to them than their own life, and they will take great pains to make him happy.

The English had never seen an Indian munshi before, but only lascars from Chittagong and Dhaka, and were consequently unacquainted with the clothes and manners of an Indian gentleman. They took me for a great man of Bengal, perhaps the brother of a Nawab, and came from far and near to see me. Whenever I went abroad crowds accompanied me, and people craned their heads out of windows and gazed at me in wonder. Children and adolescents took me for a curious specimen and ran into their houses crying, 'Look! Look! A black man is walking down the street!' – at which their elders would rush to the door and stare at me in amazement. Many children and small boys took me for a black devil and kept away in fear.

It was the height of summer, so I would go out dressed in pyjama-trousers and a long, loose shirt, with a cummerbund which held a dagger; a shawl thrown over the shoulder; turban; and gilt-embroidered shoes. Many were pleased with my costume, but others thought it was effeminate.

Within a couple of months everyone in the neighbourhood became friendly. The fear which some had felt vanished completely, and they would now jest with me familiarly. The ladies of the bazaar approached me and, smiling, said, 'Come, my dear, and kiss me!'

CHAPTER VI

LONDON

What can I say in praise of London? There is no city on earth as large or beautiful, and it is beyond my powers to describe it fittingly.

Like Calcutta it straddles a river that falls into the sea. The distance from London to the sea is roughly the distance between Calcutta and Hooghly, about three days' journey. Sea-going ships sail up river and anchor at the City ghat in front of the East India Company Headquarters, about four miles from the royal palace. (The 'City' is London's commercial district, where merchants and tradesmen have their businesses).

Not far from the City is the ancient fort known as the Tower. It is built of black stone and is very strong. Its many armouries contain a large number of cannons of brass and gun-metal, both plain and ornamented. It also has many flags and standards of Spain and France, which like many of the guns, were captured in sea and land engagements and are preserved as mementoes.

The largest gun is quite spectacular: 16 cubits long, and so large in diameter that if two persons sit down on either side they won't be able to see each other. The muzzle is so broad that a tailor of medium build can easily sit in it and work with needle and thread. I was told that once a fallen woman, who was with child, and wished to hide her shame from the world, lived for a whole year in the muzzle of the gun and bore the child there. Her lover brought her food and drink at night, and no one found her out.

People say the gun was made in Scotland, where it was part of the battery at Edinburgh Castle. When Scotland came under the English king it was transported to the Tower. I had heard descriptions of

of the wealthy are not distinguished from the remains of the poor.

The exterior of the King's palace is neither magnificent nor beautiful. The outer walls are not even plastered. It could easily be passed off as the multi-storeyed residence of a merchant of Benares. All the mansions in the city are of this sort, but the Queen's palace is very handsome. I was told, however, that the interior of the King's palace is very elegant, and that the suites of rooms and the chambers of the harem are painted an attractive verdigris.

The King's garden, which is outside the city, is very old. It has pleasant walks, lawns, and neatly arranged beds of various shapes – triangles, squares, hexagons and octagons. These are planted with varieties of flowers, green plants, and fruit trees such as the apple, gooseberry, peach, pear, filbert, etc. The garden also uses a special method to grow Indian fruits like the musk-melon, watermelon, cucumber, orange and pomegranate, and Indian flowers like the rose, henna, marigold, tuberose and the cock's-comb flower.

The cold weather in Europe doesn't allow one to grow Indian fruits and flowers in the open. A special kind of house is constructed for the purpose, three sides of which are of brick, while the fourth, which faces south, is made of glass-plates that keep out the cold air but let in the sun's rays. In the cold season stoves are lit in the house for heat, and fruit and flower seeds are sown in troughs filled with mould. The heat of the stoves and the warmth of the sunlight combine to aid the growth of Indian plants. European gardeners grow Eastern fruits in this manner and make a very good profit, charging as much as five rupees for a pomegranate and three for a musk-melon.

The trees along the walks in the King's garden are arranged very tastefully. By cutting the branches many of them have been shaped into human forms, so that at night one may mistake them for real people. It takes many days of work to tailor the trees into these shapes.

The road in front of the Queen's Palace is very broad and charming. On one side is the palace, on the other a pond which is part of a park. Deer are kept in the park and the walks in it are lined with shady walnut trees. On Sundays, men and women old and young, rich and poor, natives and foreigners, all come here to stroll and amuse themselves. In these delightful surroundings a heavy heart is automatically lightened. Sauntering courtesans with lissom figures and amorous maidens with the faces of houris spread a heavenly aura and the visitor's soul becomes a flowering garden. These fairy-faced ravishers of the heart move with a thousand blandishments and coquetries; the earth is transformed into a paradise, and heaven itself hangs down its head in shame at seeing such beauty. Men meet their fairy-like sweethearts and make love without fear of rivals or the Police, unlike India, where the *Kotwal* [Police Chief] is also a cruel guardian of public morals; and gallants can sate their eyes on rosy cheeks. As soon as I saw this place I involuntarily exclaimed:

> If there's a heaven on the face of the earth,
> It is this! It is this! It is this!

Brick buildings in Bengal have rooms with high ceilings and large doors and windows, so that there is a soothing current of air in hot weather. It is exactly opposite in Europe. There is extreme cold, frost and snow; the ceilings are low, and the doors and windows small. The roofs are not flat like the roofs of brick buildings in India. Wooden beams and planks are used to build the frame of the roof in the shape of a camel's hump; that is to say, like the slanting thatched roofs of huts in Bengal. But whereas the latter are slightly curved at the end, both slanted halves of European roofs are plain. The frame is then covered with tiles of fired clay or slate. Such roofs last up to two hundred years without repairs, and if they are still intact when the walls have decayed, can be re-utilised. The bricks in the walls are laid with mortar prepared from pulverised stones. Human hair is mixed with the mortar to give added strength to the structure. Houses may be as tall as seven, eight or nine stories, yet the walls are not thicker than a cubit. Consequently the entire building quivers if the wind rises, and strangers may fear for their safety. But there is in reality no cause for fear, though I myself was at first alarmed. The inside walls, instead of being plastered, are lined with wooden planks, which are covered with paper decorated with pretty designs in many colours.

Teak and *sal* are foreign to Vilayet; houses and ships are built here with oak and walnut. These are light in colour, very sturdy and resistant to white ants and other insects. That is why buildings last so long in this country. Mahogany and ebony, used for making chests and other household articles, are imported from China and America.

Beneath the ground floors of houses are underground chambers where bottles of wine and discarded items are stored.

The bazaars and streets of London are spacious and well-planned. Examples of such streets can be seen nowadays in parts of Calcutta. They are straight as the flight of an arrow or gunshot, and are lined with houses three to five stories tall. The ground floors are rented out as shops, the first and second floors are the owners' living quarters, and the fourth floor is the servants' quarters. Every shop has a large glass window that affords passers-by a view of the merchandise arranged inside in glass-cases. The doors have to be kept shut against the cold. When a customer knocks on the door the shopkeeper lets him in so that transactions may be made.

The houses stand in an undeviating straight line and look very much alike, like the newly built Calcutta barracks. To help strangers find the addresses they are looking for each householder has his name engraved in bronze or copper on his door and, hanging above it, a sign indicating his profession or trade. Thus a shoemaker will hang a miniature shoe and a baker a loaf of bread. If the house belongs to a prostitute her portrait, excitingly décolleté, is hung, together with her name, age and price.

The streets are paved with stone and are broad enough for three carriages driving abreast. Besides, on both sides, a smooth space about two and a half yards wide has been raised a span above the road surface using a mixture of stone chips and mortar, and set aside for pedestrians. Wooden railings, such as one may see around Calcutta's Laldighi maidan mark off the pedestrians' walks. These are interrupted in places by wooden posts revolving like wheels, called turnstiles, which allow access to pedestrians but not to carriages or horsemen.

At intervals of thirty cubits on both sides of the streets, iron-framed glass balloons are suspended at a height of eight or nine cubits from iron posts or bars projecting from shop walls. In each district of the city two men are appointed, one to clean the glass balloons by day and to put wicks and oil in them, the other to go torch in hand in the evening to light the lamps. Up to a distance of an arrow's flight the eye can see the streets and bazaars gleaming brightly. In this way streets throughout the city are lighted up. People of all classes walk about without the help of torches or lanterns till the second watch of the night. Even women of respectable families go out alone on foot to shop or visit friends and relatives till the fourth hour of darkness – but no later, for the peddlers of flesh have begun to take to the streets before dusk. In the later hours they are the only females abroad on foot, and gentlewomen stay off the streets to avoid the drunken advances of men on the prowl.

I learned that a two-crore rupee project had been completed to supply drinking water to every house in London. Channels constructed with black stone quarried in Scotland and other mountainous lands carried water from distant springs to fill up a large rectangular reservoir south of the city. Underground pipes of lead and alloys carry the water to every street, and auxiliary pipes lead off from there into tanks in every house and building. As the water is released for distribution once a week, each householder stores enough to last till the next week. In addition, every house has a well which can be tapped when water pipes freeze over in very cold weather. Many tank up enough water to last two weeks, before a cold spell starts, which they can easily tide over because it never lasts longer.

Houses in Britain do not have septic tanks. Drains running along the sides of streets carry sewage down to the sea. Anyone throwing refuse into the street is liable to be fined five rupees. In every house a hole is dug for refuse and the excrement of domestic animals. Each week a refuse collector comes with his cart and buys the refuse for two or three pice. He lets it rot in a pile and then farmers buy it from him to manure their fields. This way of keeping houses, streets, alleys and bazaars clean and tidy may be observed in the British settlements in India.

CHAPTER VII

LONDON ENTERTAINMENTS

The British Museum is a palatial building in which specimens of every conceivable extraordinary thing from the world over are preserved, so that persons with scientific interests may study their external forms and an ignorant mortal like myself may gaze at them and marvel at the diversity in nature and civilisation.

Among the many things I saw were books such as the Vedas and other Hindu scriptures written in the Nagri, Bengali and Deccanese scripts; treatises in Arabic, Greek, Syrian, Chinese; the Persian Zend Avesta, which is the holy book of Zoroastrian fire-worshippers; divers specimens of metals and gems, e.g. rubies, emeralds, turquoises, cornelians, coral, pearls, beads – both real and counterfeit – and diamonds.

There was one diamond weighing half a pound, which a governor of Madras had bought in the rough state, and on its turning out to be of the first water, presented to the King, and got preferment as a result. Europeans had never before seen such a large diamond.

I saw varieties of marble, crystal, Jesus-stone, Moses stone, jasper, amber, lodestone; different marine specimens, such as the oyster, in whose belly pearls grow, and coral, which grows like a shrub at the bottom of the sea. Divers hack off its branches and bring them up.

I was told that things immersed for many days in certain parts of the sea became petrified, such as a bottle that I saw, which had been brought up by divers from a century-old wreck; half of it was still glass, but the other half had the appearance of stone. Likewise, there were leaves of trees which had been under water and had turned into stone. If the stone was split distinct impressions of the original leaf could be seen on both halves.

There was a picture of a European woman whose forehead had sprouted a pair of horns equal in length to two fingers.

There were various things from India: musical instruments like *dholaks* [drums], timbrels, *surmandal* [a lute-like instrument]; *manduls* and *mirdung*; the crooked bamboo pole by which a palanquin is suspended; fruits peculiar to India, like mango, preserved in spirits; also preserved in spirits were snakes, e.g. the black snake, *kioonta, gokhra, dhonda, hulleela, wida, hema, turas, boora*; scorpions, dried; dried insects, like different kinds of flies, mosquitoes, fireflies, other volant insects, both of land and water, both large and small. Indeed, all the insects to be seen in India are collected here.

There were stuffed creatures, e.g. many different species of quadrupeds, like the musk deer and wild ass; birds, such as the eagle, parrot, mynah, falcon, hawk, *looree, joora, beesrak*; the *bhoj-putter*, which is the tree whose bark is used to make hookah-snakes. There was a cutting of it seven or eight cubits long as thick as a palm-tree, and with bark thin as onion-skin.

Among other interesting things were 3,000 year old mummies from Egypt.

It was the custom in ancient Egypt that when a great man died his kinsmen embalmed the body with varnish and spices and kept it rolled in cloth and the leaves of certain trees. If at a later time they wished to see the face of the dead and opened the mummy the cheeks would be found as fresh as ever. But care had to be taken so that air didn't come in contact with the body, for in that case it would putrefy instantly. Properly kept, a mummified dead body will be preserved fresh for thousands of years. The process of mummification, of course, costs thousands of rupees.

There were fish of the sea-unicorn species, with horns of varying length; the sawfish, from whose horn handles of knives and daggers can be made; the horn of a very large fish, which was twisted like the horns of the black antelope. On measuring it I found it to be five cubits long. Its thickness was that of an ordinary bamboo, but it was so heavy that I had difficulty in lifting it, even though I used both hands.

I saw the head and jawbones of a whale. They were so large that it was mind-boggling to contemplate the likely size of the whole fish. The head was shaped like that of an elephant, and the mouth, which resembled that of a cow, was larger than a man's height. It seemed that if the fish opened its mouth an elephant could easily enter it. The whale is hunted in the following manner:

North of England, at a distance of three months' journey is a place where it is dark night for nine months of the year and broad daylight for the remaining three months. The hat-wearing Englishmen go there in the dark months to hunt the whale. The intense cold has frozen the surface of the sea into a smooth sheet. Wherever there is a whale its fins pierce the frozen surface and can be seen from a distance, especially if the moon is out. As soon as they spot a whale, the hunters hurry towards it and, after breaking the surface with pickaxes, pierce its eyes with a poisoned dart to which is fixed a rope or chain whose other end is attached to a wheel shaped like that on a fishing rod. The hunters also pierce the whale's back in a few places and then retreat to their ship. In the agony caused by the wounds and, more particularly, by the action of the poison, the whale sets off in frantic motion, crumbling the ice like so much *papadom* and dragging the ship behind it for twenty to twenty-five miles, before it dies. The hunters fall on the dead giant with knives and daggers and dismember it into manageable portions. These are hauled aboard and boiled in vats to obtain oil, which is brought to England and sold to be used for various purposes, e.g. as fuel in lanterns. The whale bones are used for fashioning fancy boxes, gun butts and dagger handles.

I was told that the poison used to kill the whale is nothing but the common turmeric. Truly, one creature's food is another creature's poison!

In Vilayet the arrangements for performances of music and dance are very different from those in India. In our country the idle rich hire professional singers and dancers for private performances in their homes, where they invite their cronies. This practice is quite alien to Vilayet, where a group of impresarios jointly form a company and build a huge performing hall, or theatre, in which they put on public shows. They hire highly paid singers and dancers of both sexes, and musicians who have been trained to perfection by rare maestros, to put on their song-and-dance *tamasha* [show] decked in expensive costumes and jewellery, before an audience that includes both rich and poor Londoners, and even the emirs of the land, the princes of the realm, sometimes the King himself. The entry fee varies with the quality of the seat. The very best, set aside for emirs and princes, cost one *ashrafi* [gold sovereign] each; those of the middle rank, for gentlemen, cost five rupees each; and those for common citizens cost eight annas each. Attendance at a performance may be as high as thousands. But the important point is that gentlemen (for only five rupees) and ordinary citizens (for only eight annas) can sit together in peace and comfort and enjoy a performance fit for royalty, the like of which people in India haven't even seen in dreams; and thereby the performers earn thousands of rupees every day. Truly, the Firinghees can accomplish great things at little expense. In India, on the other hand, luxurious young men squander a couple of hundred rupees on an evening's nautch party; and lakhs of rupees of patrimony, which they may inherit, take wing in a short time.

In Vilayet, when a spectator pays the entry fee he is given a slip of paper on which the class of his seat is mentioned. When he produces this slip at the entrance he is let in and directed to the appropriate section of the hall. Charming music from violins and guitars, many strange dramatic pieces, curtains of many colours, antics of *habshi* performers, dancers lovely as houris – all these make a highly entertaining spectacle.

My pen lacks the ability not only to describe properly the many interesting things I heard and saw in such performances, but even to write a short panegyric. Of all the spectacles, that of the curtains of seven colours is quite wonderful, for every instant the scene changes and a new painting is exhibited. Then people disguised as angels and fairies appear on stage and dance, and then suddenly disappear. There is an elusive man with a black face, a kind of devil, called Harlequin, who appears and then hides himself, and sometimes attaches himself to the dancing-girls, taking them by the hand and dancing with them, then scampers off and leaps through the window. At seeing his antics I laughed very heartily.

Talking is not allowed in the Theatre. Though the audience is large, there is no noise or clamour. When they are pleased by a performance, instead of shouting *Shabash!* [Bravo!] or *Wah! Wah!*

[Wonderful!] as we do in India, they stamp on the floor or clap their hands.

I saw many plays performed, one of which was based on the following story. A Captain's wife discovers that her husband is a bigamist. She raises a great clamour, and in a mighty rage lays her complaint before a court of law. Since bigamy is a capital offence in this country, the judge sentences the man to death. The plaintiff, who in her years of intimacy with her husband has become deeply attached to him, is torn with remorse and vows to die with him. She accompanies him to the place of execution, crying and beating her head and breast all the while. The second wife, her heart on fire, walks on the other side of the man, who looks as pale as a corpse as he proceeds on the road to death. At the place of execution such intense grief is displayed as I am unable to describe. In the end the judges, on the King's recommendation, pardon the Captain.

A couple of miles south of the King's palace, in the area known as Chelsea, there lives a horseman unrivalled in his profession, who in skill surpasses the legendary Krishna or Rustum. His trick-riding is so impressive that people flock to see him perform. His house, known as the Circus, stands on a *bigha* of land, part of which had been levelled to allow horses and chariots to manoeuvre. Here he puts on his show to the delight of a large audience. The entry fee is one rupee.

In the performance that I had the opportunity to witness, a horse was brought in and with a touch of the whip made to gallop. The horseman leapt on to its back, and springing up stood upright, then stood on one leg and turned round. All this while the horse kept galloping swiftly in a circle. The rider then danced on the horse's back and wheeled round. Sometimes he lay supine on its back, at other times he stood erect; at one moment he stooped down; at another, he stood on his head and threw his heels in the air, beating time with his feet; and sometimes, lifting his hands from the saddle he clapped them and kept time with both hands and feet. Again, placing both hands on the saddle, he tumbled over.

But the most entertaining part of the exhibition was when he seized a coin with his lips and lifted it from the ground. In Vilayet, we should remember, coins are very small, The *chabook sowars*, or horse-breakers, of India, can pick up coins with the hand, which is nothing compared to this. After this feat a second horse was introduced and while the two galloped side by side, the horseman danced and turned round, sometimes on one and sometimes on the other. Then a third horse was introduced and he danced on all three in the same way. He then leapt over the three horses from one side and landed on the ground on his feet on the other side.

Next he placed a bar and leapt over it on a horse. The bar was then raised, but this time the horse failed to clear it and both rider and mount came tumbling down. It was a severe fall, but the horseman sprang up instantly, as if it was but a trifle, and quickly remounted, so that none might say his horsemanship was defective. He seemed a little annoyed with the horse for its lack of vigour and punished it slightly. Then after galloping once round the Circus he attempted the leap again, this time clearing the bar with ease. The spectators applauded warmly.

Among the other tricks presented in the Circus was the following conjuring trick. A wooden duck was set afloat in a small copper cistern, around whose rim the letters of the alphabet were displayed. At a sign from the conjuror the duck turned its head towards him and approaching the side of the cistern where he stood, remained there. The conjuror then asked the name of someone in the audience. At once the duck began to swim about and spell the name by dabbing at relevant letters with its beak. I surmise that the trick exploits the innate property of the lodestone. A piece of steel was probably concealed in the body of the duck, and the juggler had a piece of lodestone in his hand, so the duck automatically moved in whichever direction he gestured.

To the south-west of the metropolis, on the other side of the Thames, is a large garden with lovely tree-lined walks and, at intervals, wooden pavilions of various shapes– triangular, round rectangular or octagonal – containing statuary festooned with creepers. In the centre of the garden is a house where there is music and dancing. Celebrated singers perform here to warm applause. In the recesses of the garden there are arbours, in one of which there are many pictures depicting men and women and, in some cases, beautiful, bewinged fairies. There is also an accurate representation of the scene after the defeat of Nawab Siraj-ud-dowla at Plassey; it shows Nawab Mir Zafar Ali Khan, Lord Clive and the English officers embracing each other and shaking hands. Elsewhere in the garden there are wonderful displays of fireworks and cascades.

Near the bazaar called Haymarket there was an exhibition of a giantess. Those who wanted to see her had each to pay a fee of a rupee. As soon as she heard that a dark-skinned Indian man had come to see her, she came laughing towards me. She stood well over five cubits in height. When I stood before her I only reached up to her armpit. Her figure was stout in proportion to her height; her wrist was thicker than mine, and in physical strength she was like a champion. Her face was so beautiful and her figure so desirable, that neither my pen nor my tongue is adequate to sing the praises of her fairness. We stared at each other for a while. Having never seen an Indian man dressed as I was, she contemplated me with wonder; and I, seeing her resplendent features and magnificent form, was quite confounded

CHAPTER VIII

THE MADRASSAH OF OXFORD

After three months in one place one naturally grows an attachment for it, and so it was with grief and sorrow that I left London, and accompanied by Captain Swinton arrived at Oxford. But on seeing this beautiful city dejection gave way to gladness, and the bird of joy built a nest on the bough of my heart.

Oxford is three stages away from London and is the seat of an ancient *madrassah* [school]. It has many old churches, some of which date over a millennium, yet appear newly built. The walls are mostly dark stone and the roofs, covered with sheets of lead, are totally impervious to rain. I was particularly impressed by a massive building whose roof was not supported by a single beam or pillar – it was entirely terraced over – yet suffered no damage in even the harshest tempest. There are many old gardens, laid out with pleasant walks, flower-beds, arbours and pools of water. The branches of trees and plants are cut to form accurate representations of human beings, quadrupeds and cottages, which are curiously charming; they are the result of lifelong devotion by expert gardeners.

In one of the colleges of the *madrassah* I met a professor called Dr. Hunt, who showed me many Persian works in the college library, among them a translation of the Arabic *Kaleelah wa Dumnah* ['Kaleelah and Dumnah', an 8th Century translation of a collection of Sanskrit fables, *Panchatantra*]. From this library I copied out the epilogue of the *Ferhung Jehangaree* [a 17th Century Persian dictionary] for Captain Swinton.

I also met Mr. Jones, now a Judge of the Calcutta High Court, who together with Captain Swinton took me on a round of the libraries in Oxford, where they showed me many Arabic, Turkish and Persian works. There was a letter in Persian and Turkish, which a Turkish potentate named Moolekul Joosea had sent to the English King. As no one in England knew these languages well, many parts of the letter had remained unexplicated. I had no difficulty in explaining its purport to my companions. Then they put other books in my hand, with the intention of testing my knowledge, and I read out passages from them and explained them to their satisfaction.

During our voyage to Europe Captain Swinton with my help read the whole of the *Kuleelah wa Dumnah* and translated into English the section of the *Ferhung Jehangaree* that sets out the twelve rules comprising the grammar of the Persian language. Mr. Jones saw that translation and with Captain Swinton's permission used it in compiling his Persian grammar, which has brought him fame and money.

One of the libraries contained many superb statues and pictures by old masters. These had been purchased from abroad, some for as much as ten to twenty thousand rupees. Most of the statues of men and women in marble are from Greece and Egypt, and are five, six, or seven cubits in height. Who knows, perhaps our distant ancestors were of such lofty stature!

Though I am no judge of sculpture, I could not but be impressed by the lifelike features, figures, postures and expressions of these statues. Their creators have surpassed Mani and Behzad. Though England now leads Europe in education and the arts, I heard that even her contemporary artists are no match for the ancient masters.

I was told of a great artist of ancient Egypt, four of whose paintings were renowned the world over. When the Persian King declared a war of vengeance against the Jews for persecuting the prophet Yahya [John the Baptist], and sacked their cities, many Greek works of art were either destroyed or scattered. With them one of these four paintings was also lost. The Europeans have made an extensive search for it and have offered rewards ranging from one to three rupees for anyone finding it, but to no avail. The remaining three thousand pictures by the artist are now in Europe.

Once upon a time in England there was a painter who had no equal among his contemporaries. One day he hired a poor man into his house and drugged him senseless. He then stood the man against a wall and bound his feet and outstretched arms to nails driven into the wall. When the man regained consciousness the artist stabbed him in the chest with a sharp knife, and while he was in his death throes, made an accurate painting of his tortured expression and convulsed limbs. Never before had such a convincing picture of mortal agony been painted. Connoisseurs had nothing but praise for it. However, the murder of the innocent man did not remain long concealed and the murderer was tried and sentenced to death. When asked to make a last request before the execution was to be carried out, he said, 'My picture is still a little unfinished. I would like to add a few final brush strokes.'

The request was granted and picture and painting materials brought to the artist. To everyone's horror he quickly painted it over with black ink. They began to lament that a unique work of art had been destroyed.

The execution was postponed and the painter brought before the King, who demanded an explanation for his extraordinary behaviour.

The painter replied, 'I took great pains to paint that picture, but if I am to lose my life for it, what good will its preservation do me?'

'And if we spare your life,' said the King, 'will you be able to restore the painting to its original state?'

'Certainly,' replied the painter. 'For every problem there is a solution, just as every lock has a key.'

On the King's assurance of reprieve the painter set to restoring the picture. He had cunningly applied a black tint that is slow to penetrate canvas. Now using a chemical process known only to himself he quickly removed all traces of it. The onlookers were amazed and declared he was the greatest master of his art.

The English hold artists in such high regard that they are prepared to spend lakhs of rupees for a painting or a drawing on paper – or, as we have seen, pardon a murder by an artist of genius. If they notice signs of talent in an artist they reward him generously and accord him a place among the eminent citizens of the land. It would be surprising if knowledge and the arts didn't flourish in this country.

In India, by contrast, even if one devotes all of one's life to learning and the arts, and is acknowledged the world's greatest master in these fields, the leaders of society will not pay him any respect; rather they will despise and condemn him, and he will acquire neither fame nor fortune and will die in misery. Under such circumstances it is a wonder that anyone at all should apply himself to the sciences and arts.

I visited an observatory at Oxford. It is nearly a thousand cubits tall and five hundred cubits broad, and is built of black and white stones. It is vertically divided into a round part and an octagonal part. There are nine stories in all, each containing many books on physics, astronomy and astrology. A dome on top, set with glass windows, lets in light which, through holes about a span in diameter in each floor, trickles down to the lowest storey. Scientists climb to the top of the building and contemplate the seven heavens through a huge telescope, determine the position and speed of the planets and stars, and investigate their influence on each of the twelve zodiacal signs.

I was taken to a physics laboratory and shown a complete wooden model of the earth and the sky. The seventh heaven enclosed the other six, and it was indicated that each of them is separated from the next by a space of five miles. The popular notion that the seven heavens are like curtains lying one on top of another is therefore erroneous. English scientists argue that if this were the case, as there would be no space between them, the stars of the upper heavens would not have been visible from earth. Whatever doubts I had regarding this theory vanished when I saw the model of the universe.

The earth is an egg-like sphere that hangs in the space enclosed by the heavens and revolves like a wheel on an axis represented by a wooden pin. In each moment the earth rotates 360 times on its axis and in each year it completes a vertical revolution. Maps of the seven great geographic regions of the world were hung around the model of the universe.

People of all countries can see the sun, moon, planets and stars, because the earth is hanging in space. It also stands to reason that in every country people should think they are standing on top of the world, and that other countries are situated beneath them.

Whenever, owing to its rotation, the earth comes into alignment with a zodiacal sign it is said to be in that sign. Likewise, when the shadow of the sun, moon or a star is seen from earth to fall on a zodiacal sign it is said to be in that sign. In this manner the heavenly bodies are constantly moving from one sign to another. Among them the swiftest in rotation is the moon, which rotates 360 times a minute;

once a month it enters the same sign with the sun. I should mention, though, that Persian and Firinghee scientists hold opposite views regarding the motion of the earth and the heavenly bodies. But without knowledge of science one cannot even try to resolve the controversy.

In this laboratory I also saw an astrolabe. It was circular in shape and had astrological markings, with whose help it is possible to determine auspicious times.

In a medical college in Oxford I saw a complete human skeleton suspended from the ceiling; the limbs and joints were secured with iron wires and nails.

CHAPTER IX

SCOTLAND

Captain Swinton and I left Oxford for Scotland in winter. This was when I saw snow for the first time. It is like *abeer*, the powder Hindus sprinkle on each other at the Holi festival, only instead of being coloured it is a brilliant white. It falls from the sky like dust blown by the wind and covers the ground, hills, houses, trees, bushes, rivers and lakes like molten wax.

When the cold becomes very intense the water in rivers, lakes and canals freezes into hard ice, which is smooth and white as marble, or like a sheet of crystal or glass. The water may freeze to a depth of five or ten cubits, in which case pedestrians, horsemen, carriages, loaded wagons and even elephants can easily cross over it.

Sometimes snowfall is so heavy that streets and alleys are covered knee-deep overnight. Then in the morning householders have to set their servants to work with spades and shovels to clear a path in front of their doors. In the country the snow fills up ditches and hollows, so that they become impossible to distinguish from level ground. This makes travel dangerous. The common roads can be recognised by the tracks made day and night by carters and wagoneers. But if for some reason, be it the will of God, human error, or drunkenness, a person is not able to distinguish the road he may come to a bad end. When excessive snowfall covers roads, ditches and fields like a sheet of white glass, and there is no sign of the road, carriages, horses and loaded wagons can easily slip into deep pits, causing deaths. Such an accident occurred near Oxford that year when a loaded dray with thirteen men and four horses fell into a pit. Only the drayman managed to leap to safety; all the others perished.

On our journey I observed people travelling on the ice in an amazing manner. I was told that they could cover as much as twenty miles an hour. I had heard stories of this means of travel from sahibs in India but it seemed so extraordinary that I couldn't believe them. Now that I saw it myself my doubts vanished.

The manner in which these people travel on ice is as follows: wooden soles, like the wooden slippers [*Khadam*] of India, are taken. To the middle of the wood is attached a piece of polished steel one span in length and of half a finger's breadth. The whole is attached tightly to the foot with leather straps. When the person stands up the piece of steel is straight upon the ice. If the foot slips or is bent to one side the person will fall down. It takes some practice even to stand up in these shoes. But with frequent exercise it is possible to acquire the ability to glide along swiftly and to turn in any direction, as I had the pleasure of witnessing. When they passed me by their speed was greater than that of the wind or an arrow or a swift bird. As they glided along in their white robes the Europeans appeared like angels who had descended on earth and were moving about, or like spirits risen from the dead and gliding about. One moment they glided into view; the next moment vanished from sight.

I was told that the people of Holland, both men and women, excelled at this exercise, because their country is scored by numerous streams which freeze over in winter and allow them ample scope to practise it. During the season of frost and ice, the poor villagers of Holland carry milk-pails, jars of oil, baskets of fruits and vegetables on their heads and shoulders, make a circuit of the towns and cities from morning till noon and, when their produce has all been sold, return home across distances of up to 150 miles. Incredibly, not a drop of the milk or oil is spilt in the process.

After a short time we arrived in Scotland, which is directly to the north of England. The country is divided into lowlands and highlands, the latter being far to the north. Mountains and forests abound in Scotland; consequently the population is relatively sparse and towns and cities fewer than in England. The number of wealthy people, too, is comparatively small. But change is in the air. Since Scotland is now united with England, the Scotch have more opportunities in business, banking and in the service of the government and the East India Company, and the wealth and size of the Scottish cities is on the increase. It is only natural that this should be so, for friendship between two peoples increases the wealth of both, while enmity begets poverty.

For centuries Scotland was a separate kingdom, frequently in conflict with England, and as a result the citizens of both countries were continually harassed. But a century and a half ago, when Queen Elizabeth died without leaving an heir, the English installed the Scottish king as Sovereign of the throne and crown of England, and he ruled over both countries. From then onwards the two countries have been united into one kingdom.

The Scots are an abstemious, hard-working and brave people and consider themselves superior to the English, who, they say, are gluttonous and cowardly. The English, on the other hand, account themselves superior in wealth and education and despise the Scotch as being poor and stupid. Though English is the language of both countries it differs from one to the other in a few terms.

The capital of Scotland is Edinburgh. It has an ancient citadel standing on a hill, well out of range of the cannons of likely invaders. Within it is a wooden-roofed, white marble building that is quite beautiful.

In Edinburgh we put up at the house of Captain Swinton's father. Captain Swinton introduced me to his parents, both of whom were about eighty years old. They had five children: three sons, the eldest of whom was called John, and two grown-up daughters, both spinsters.

In Vilayet a marriage is contracted through the mutual consent of man and woman. Ideally, the man should be good-looking, of an agreeable temper and with an income, whether inherited or earned in business or employment. The woman likewise should be attractive, of a good disposition, well-versed in at least some of the fine arts, and with a portion either from her father or former husband. It is relatively rare and a truly fortunate match where all these good qualities are present. Some people, however, look only to wealth. If a woman is both ugly and poor, none will have her, for Vilayet is the emporium of beauty, where women of surpassing loveliness are common, and wealthy and virtuous ones are not hard to find. Consequently there are thousands of old women who have never seen the face of a husband.

Here is yet another example of the truth that excellencies that abound in a country are depreciated while ordinary articles that are rare but of no value in their country of origin are very dear. Thus tamarinds sell for a pice a seer in India, and in Vilayet for one *ashrafi* or more.

With old age Captain Swinton's father became soft in the head and began squandering his fortune so that his eldest son John, in accordance with the practice in this country in such cases, laid the matter before the court. The judges, following the custom of the land, decided to put a stop to the old man's irresponsible behaviour by depriving him of the management of his estate, which they now entrusted to his heir, the eldest son, with the stipulation that he should allot to his father whatever was requisite to keep him in comfort. The arrangement worked well, as I saw with my own eyes. Mr. Swinton senior, though superannuated, lived a pleasant life, devoting himself to painting and other hobbies.

I learned that Captain Swinton had trained as a surgeon and acquired considerable expertise in the field. In order to study the functioning of the veins and arteries he subjected a poor man to vivisection, which led to that man's death. But soon word of the crime was out and for fear of his life he fled the country by ship, reaching Malacca and Pegu, where for some years he practised as a surgeon. From there he went to Madras and accompanied Colonel Clive to Calcutta at the time of the war with Nawab Siraj-ud-Dowlah. He went to Azimabad and enrolled in the Company's army with the rank of Captain. He commanded a battalion of sepoys and as a companion in arms of Colonel Carmac distinguished himself in many battles. With a single battalion he achieved the conquest of Teera and Roushanabad. Serving under Major Adams in the wars against Nawab Mir Kasim Ali Khan he fought with distinction in the battles of Monghyr and Azimabad. As a member of the English Army under Colonel Carnac that aided the Great Moghul, Badshah Shah Alam, Captain Swinton took part in the subjugation of Kali and Kora-Jahanabad, and subsequently he was the Colonel's aide in the talks that led to a treaty with Nawab Shuja-ud-Dowla of Oudh. Finally, at the insistence of Badshah Shah Alam, the Captain accompanied the present author to Europe on the mission described at the outset.

The Swintons trace their descent from a redoubtable hero of yore who once bagged a white boar at a hunt, and as the generic English word for the species is 'swine' was named Swinton after his prize. His descendants adopted this as their family name. It is the custom of the land that every nobleman and eminent citizen has a seal engraved with his ancestral arms, which is also displayed on his belongings – e.g. his carriage and books – so that the identity of his family may be known. On the seals of the Swintons I noticed, beside a shield and certain weapons, the figure of a white boar, from which people might recognise their owners as descendants of the original swine-hunter.

With the increase of descendants a family divides into many branches and to distinguish between these other distinctive marks are added to the original coat of arms i.e. the label, crescent, martlets, etc. of the different sons. But all these branches retain the surname of the founder of the family, along with which they have a given name, e.g. John Swinton, Charles Swinton, Archibald Swinton.

Every Scottish family of note possesses books setting out in detail the histories of their clans. The scions of these families consider honour and dignity their birthright and despise those of humble origin whom they treat like menials. Even if people of humble birth have risen to wealth through individual effort, the humble employment of their forebears is cast up to them; they are ridiculed as the sons of shoemakers, barbers, cotton-spinners, etc.

CHAPTER X

THE HIGHLANDS

The Highlands occupy the northern extremity of Scotland. Further to its north is the sea. It is sparsely populated, being infertile and full of mountains and forests. It snows and rains virtually twelve months a year. But this harsh climate doesn't seem to inconvenience the inhabitants, especially the lower orders, who have grown used to it. When a shepherd or farmer feels tired in the course of work he will spread half of his cloak on the bare ground, and lying down on it, cover himself with the other half and go to sleep. If so much snow collects on the cloak that they feel suffocated, they spring up, give it a shake and lie down again on the snow.

The tails and wool of the sheep are curled like the cotton of a coverlet. For this reason the cold cannot penetrate into their bodies and throughout the year the flocks can be kept out to pasture. When snow covers the ground and grazing becomes impossible, the sheep as well as horses and cows are fed upon hay. Sheep on whose bodies wool is scant grow weak and thin in a severe winter, but such specimens are rare. The grass here is sweet and extremely nutritive for animals. Grams and pulses do not grow in Vilayet, but there is a grain with blackish seeds called corn, which the Scotch eat themselves and also feed their animals.

The Highlanders wear a jacket and a cap, but neither breeches nor boots. The lower part of the body is covered by a skirt called a kilt, but the knee is bare and cotton stockings are worn on the legs. Instead of shoes they wear wooden sandals fastened to the feet with leather straps. They carry a double-edged sword. I was told that their courage was beyond compare. But they are also simple-minded and doltish.

A Highlander who had gone to London was sightseeing about the bazaars, followed by a curious crowd of Englishmen and boys. One of the Englishmen in sport lifted the skirt of the Highlander's kilt from behind. He was overcome with shame at this, but at the same time his wrath was inflamed and with a stroke of his sword he cut off the offender's head. The Police and townspeople surrounded him but could not force him to surrender. He undauntedly stood his ground, prepared either to kill or die. He wounded many people, and on whichever side he charged they fled before him. No one had the courage to approach him, far less seize him. Word of this strange situation eventually reached the King, who sent a courtier to summon him. The Courtier went before him and said, 'His Majesty has sent for you.' On hearing the King's name the Highlander immediately bowed his head and followed the royal envoy. When he appeared in the royal presence the King asked why he had heedlessly murdered a man. The Highlander knelt on one knee, according to the custom of Vilayet, bowed his head and after making obeisance, replied in a respectful tone, 'When that man exposed a shameful part of my body I felt my honour had been ridiculed, and therefore in a state of rightful anger I struck him dead. But when I received your royal summons I hastened to surrender myself to you and I feel proud to have been permitted to kiss your threshold. Otherwise none would have been able to capture me alive.' The King was impressed by this simple and courageous man's defence and pardoned him.

There is another story in which a highlander had a comical adventure as a result of his unfamiliarity with the English language as it is spoken in London. On a visit there he was greatly distressed because of the high price of victuals. One day he met a friendly stranger in a bazaar and told him of his plight. The man asked him why he didn't go to the shop of a penny-cook, where poor people could get cheap but wholesome food. In these shops for just a couple of pice one can get a piece of bread, a portion of meat and half-a-seer of beer or barley water. But the Highlander forgot the word 'penny-cook' and thought it was 'penny-cut,' so that when he asked a passer-by where he could find it the man thought he wanted a cheap barber and pointed out a barber's shop. The Highlander went and knocked and was let in by the barber and offered a chair. The barber filled an ewer with hot water, put a lump of soap in it and after working a lather, placed it before the Highlander. Then he went upstairs to fetch his razors. The Highland mistook the sudsy water for broth and the soap for a potato and being famished polished them off without ado. When the barber came back and saw what had happened he was struck dumb with amazement. The Highlander, who didn't notice anything, calmly produced two pice from his pocket and laying it on the table said, 'I am obliged to you. The broth was very good, but the potato was insufficiently boiled.'

There are amusing stories about the English too, particularly their country people, who are ignorant and stupid. One of them went to town where he was feted by a friend. He greatly relished a sheep's liver kebab, which he had never tasted before, and took down its recipe. Before returning home he went to a butcher and bought a sheep's liver, which he tied in a napkin and carried in his hand. A pie dog came up from behind, snatched the liver, napkin and all, and scampered off. The rustic shouted jeeringly after dog, 'You silly beast, you've got the raw liver, but the recipe is in my pocket!'

Another countryman, an old farmer, intended to pay a visit to his landlord. His wife handed him a pig in a poke to take as a gift. The journey being a long one, he had to stop for the night at an inn. The landlord of the inn decided to play a prank and substituted a puppy for the pig. The following morning the unsuspecting farmer continued on his journey and reached his landlord's manor. The landlord greeted him cordially and noticing the bag asked if the farmer had brought a present for him. 'I am too poor to bring a fitting gift for you,' replied the farmer, 'but I have brought you a pig.' The landlord who knew about the man's poverty, was touched at this and said, 'From you that is a great gift indeed. Open the bag and let me see it.' The farmer opened the bag and to his amazement discovered the puppy. The landlord, suspecting a joke, flew into a rage and threw out the farmer with execrations. The poor farmer returned home the way he had come, stopping overnight at the inn. This time as he slept the landlord of the inn replaced the puppy with the pig. The next day the farmer returned home and fell on his wife, shouting. 'You bitch, you have disgraced me before the landlord. You put a puppy in the bag.' The poor woman denied the charge, and demanded proof, whereupon the farmer opened the bag and out leapt the pig. The farmer now turned on the pig, for he thought it had changed itself into a puppy and back again, and giving it a few cuts with his whip said 'You son of a bitch, I'll eat you if you play this trick on me again!'

Such stories only prove the truth that Allah did not create all five fingers equal. There is no country in the world where there are no stupid and ignorant people. In fact, everywhere they are the majority.

CHAPTER XI

ON HISTORY AND RELIGION

We learn from books of history that after the great deluge the human race sprang anew from Prophet Noah's children. For this reason Prophet Noah is called the second Adam. He had three sons – Japhet, Shem and Ham. Turks, Persians, Berbers and Tartars are descended from Japhet; Indians, Negroes and Chinese from Ham, and from Shem the Syrians and the nations under the Roman empire. With further increase in population they spread over the entire world; each region became distinguished by a particular name, its inhabitants acquired manners and customs peculiar to themselves, and there arose differences in language, in religion and in rituals.

Hazrat Ibrahim [Prophet Abraham] was descended from Shem and he had two sons; Ishmael born of Bibi Hegira, from whom sprang the Arabs and the house of Qureish, into which was born Prophet Mohammed (Peace be upon him); and Isaac, born of Bibi Sarah, from whom sprang the Israelites and many prophets including Hazrat Issa (Jesus Christ), the Syrians and those under the Roman empire. As Bibi Sarah was a princess, the Israelites maintain that they are noble on both sides and call the Arab Moslems children of a slave. Consequently there is continued strife and enmity between the Israelites and the Moslems.

The noteworthy powers in Europe are the Holy Roman Empire, Italy, Germany, Prussia, Russia, Denmark, Portugal, Holland, Spain, France, England, Turkey and three other countries whose names I do not recall at the moment. These are all monarchies, with the exception of tiny Holland, the land of the Dutch people, which is governed by its noblemen. The rest of its inhabitants are mostly affluent merchants but as the waters off their coast abound in fish there are also many fishermen and fish sellers, as a result of which other Europeans contemptuously refer to the Dutch as fishmongers. Besides, as they don't have a king they are considered mean, lacking in glory.

The Roman Empire is very old. At one time all the other Firinghee lands owed it allegiance. It contained a large megalopolis called Constantinople, which is now known as Istanbul. It is unique among cities. With the rise of Islam it came under Moslem control in the reign of Caliph Omar. It is situated on a sea beyond which lies the land of the Franks. The hat-wearing Firinghees say that Rome was once a vast kingdom. When Constantinople passed into the hands of the Moslems the remainder of the Roman empire across the sea became part of the kingdom of the Franks. The Firinghees call the Roman ruler Pope, which means Father and many of them regard him as the Prophet Christ's deputy. Time was when all the kings of Europe were subservient to him and received their royal titles from him. They would respect, honour and revere him and come to his assistance whenever needed. But things have changed. The English, for instance, differ in points of religion from the Pope and his followers and the English king does not defer to the Pope any longer.

The languages of Italy and France are sweet and elegant and they are studied by the English on this account and also because there are many classics of science and philosophy written in them without acquaintance with which one is not considered learned.

Italy, France and Germany are powerful states, but Spain is the richest of all the Firinghee nations. This is because most of the gold mines in the new world have fallen in Spanish colonies. The Spaniards have a reputation for being clever and hard-working. They may in fact be more so than even the English.

I was told that France, Italy and Germany put together equal India in area, but Russia is at least three times India's size. Indeed, in length and breadth Russia surpasses all other countries. The Russian monarch is a mighty power and his subjects are celebrated for indefatigable industry, so that the English, who are both alert and active, are regarded by them as lazy and indolent. Sheik Nizamee's history of Alexander's reign, *The Secunder Namah*, ['The Story of

Alexander'] contains an account of Russia as it was in that bygone age, when its inhabitants were rude and uncivilised. But about forty or fifty years ago their king, the Czar Peter, started sending Russians abroad to England and other countries for advanced study, so that they might on their return educate their compatriots in their special fields. I met two of these Russian scholars in Edinburgh, where they were students at the college. Their complexion was ruddy, almost brick-red.

The Russian Czar and the English king are on excellent terms. There are many English officers – Generals, Colonels, Captains – in the Russian Army, whose chief task is to instruct Russians in the manufacture of cannons and muskets, and in tactics. Many English civilians too prefer to live and work in Russia. The Russians deem the English superior to other European nations in military matters, personal bravery and intellect, and try to emulate them. They have already surpassed many other European nations in military might and political influence. A couple of years back the Russian Czar sent his army to attack Turkey and owing to the treachery of the Turkish wazir [Prime Minister] scored an initial victory and annexed a Turkish province, but through the mercy of Allah the Russians eventually suffered a defeat and were forced to retreat.

After the death of Hazrat Issa [Jesus Christ] the Caliphate and office of Imam of the Christians devolved on his twelve apostles. The Evangels which comprise the holy scriptures of the Christians were composed by them. They travelled into Syria, the Roman empire and other lands, where they propagated the Christian faith and established themselves as religious heads. In the centuries following their deaths, differences arose among the padres or Christian priests regarding the origin of their religion and rituals; diverse interpretations and commentaries on their scriptures were produced; and various sects and orders arose. These matters are touched upon in Maulana Rumi's *Masnabi,* [a 12th century Persian didactic epic].

I am no specialist in the history, beliefs and rituals of the Christians, but I learnt something about these matters from English books and translations of the Evangels, which I will summarise. At the root of Christianity is the belief that Hazrat Issa is the Son of God, which Christians claim is borne out by the fact that the Virgin Mary bore him without having known man.

Some among the English, however, do not believe this, because they think that the pure nature of God isn't born of anyone, nor can anyone be born of it. They maintain that the Almighty is unique and above the process of procreation, and it is only as a token of his divine love and kindness that he addressed Jesus as his son and exalted him above other prophets.

Another fundamental point in the Evangels, assented to by all Christians, is that after he was crucified by the Jews his body ascended to the fourth heaven and returned after three days, when he met Simon Peter and two female devotees and spoke to them the following words: 'My birth as a man, my life on earth, my death at the hands of Jews, my passion, all of these I have undergone so that all-merciful God may take account of all I have suffered and forgive all sinners on the day of Judgement. No more prophets will come after me. If anyone claims to be one, do not believe him, for he is a liar. But before the Day of Judgement, when the sun will rise in the west and set in the east, I shall return and the whole of Creation will be received into my faith.' Jesus spoke in this view for some time, then vanished into thin air. At the time, none but the twelve apostles accepted his message from beyond the grave.

All the Firinghees of Europe are Christians, but their co-religionists outside this continent are weak in number and of little account. The Christians in Syria, Turkey and other Moslem Kingdoms have to pay the jizya tax [formerly imposed on minorities in Moslem countries]. The Armenians, whose native land was once a province of the Persian empire and who are now scattered through many countries, are also Christian, though their beliefs differ significantly from those of other Christian sects. They are without homeland or king and are described by the Firinghees as a nation of slaves. Those among them who dwell in Turkey, Syria, Persia and other Moslem countries are tax-paying subjects like the native populations of those lands.

The Jews, who follow the religion of Hazrat Musa (Prophet Moses) lead a wretched existence, scattered throughout Arabia, Syria, the Roman empire and other lands. They had persecuted Hazrat Issa and finally crucified him and on this account are held to be base and contemptible. No person respects or esteems them; on the contrary, those of other faiths, including the Moslems, wish to put them to death. In many parts of Europe they live in constant terror for their lives, for if the Christians catch a Jew in their country, they burn him alive. But the English pursue a policy of tolerance and do not prevent adherents of any faith from practising their religion. In London I saw quite a few Jewish peddlers of eatables and cloths plying their trade in complete peace.

Christians do not distinguish between *haram* [forbidden] and *halal* [permitted] foods, but will eat whatever agrees with the palate and is recommended by their medical authorities, who have studied and enumerated the wholesome and harmful qualities of all comestibles.

The theological background to this practice is worth noting. The general position of Jesus Christ was that the *Torah* of Moses was valid in its entirety since it was a revealed scripture, but a particular event led to a reinterpretation of its mensal precepts. Once while travelling, Christ's disciples began eating bread without first washing themselves as prescribed in the Torah, so that the food technically became *haram*. Jewish priests, ever alert to the faults of Jesus and his flock, protested to Jesus, 'You always advise people to follow the *Torah*, and yet you have overlooked a violation of its precepts by your close disciples, who have eaten bread without washing their faces and hands either before or after.'

Jesus, whose patience was tried by the constant niggling of the Jews, retorted heatedly, 'My disciples know that in the case of mundane rituals the sin of omission is not punishable and so it is all the same whether one performs them or not. God has created the earth and all worldly objects solely for man's benefit, so man is free to consume food any way he wishes. Whatever goes down his gullet is *halal* but what comes out of his mouth can be seen as *haram*. In the latter category fall bad deeds like uttering lies and committing perjury. You condone venal sins, yet create a furore over venial ones.'

On another occasion when Jesus stopped at a village the villagers brought him a large beaker of wine. When Jesus lifted it to his lips it miraculously turned into milk, of which he drank a little and distributed the rest among his disciples, saying, 'If you can perform this miracle and turn wine into milk, you may drink as much as you please.'

On the basis of these Biblical stories Christians consider it permissible to drink wine or eat the flesh of swine. But there is a sect of Christians who refuse to eat the flesh of swine or drink wine, on the grounds that Jesus upheld the *Torah* and exhorted his followers to abide by it.

The commandments in the Evangels are briefly as follows: mankind is to consider the divinity as single; to believe in his word and in his prophets; not to bear false witness; to refrain from lying; not to commit adultery, not to kill; and to treat the poor and the neighbours like brothers.

Most Christian nations adore Jesus Christ and Bibi Mariam [Virgin Mary] like Allah; they place effigies of Christ and Mary in their churches and worship them. But the English consider such idolatry improper and keep their churches devoid of such images. They believe Allah is without form.

Every year on Christ's birthday the French make a wooden effigy of the pregnant Mary and at the time of Christ's birth draw from under her skirt a rag doll smeared in red dye, to the loud accompaniment of music and chanting. Then they seat the wooden Mary on a throne with the rag doll in her lap and reverently fall down and worship them. I witnessed such a spectacle in Mauritius where Captain Swinton and Mr. Peacock, who were with me, remarked laughingly, 'This sort of absurd behaviour can be seen among the French, the Portuguese and the Spaniards, but not among the English.'

There is much bigotry among many Christian nations. If a Moslem were to go there and give the *azan* and openly practise the rites of Islam he would be instantly burnt at the stake. But the English are free of such bigotry. Even if one were to build a mosque in England and pray and fast as Allah enjoins, no objection would be raised, for the English say, "What is it to us what the religion of another may be?" For as the common adage has it, "Jesus for his faith and Moses for his faith."

There are lakhs of wealthy, hypocritical priests among the French. It is an annual custom for French men and women to go individually to their priests to confess the sins they have committed during the year. They give their priests large gifts so that by prayer and fasting they may intercede on their behalf and obtain God's pardon. The English ridicule all this as sheer folly. 'God is the King of Kings and on the Day of Judgement he will pardon or punish as he pleases. It is ridiculous to believe he will accept the recommendation of such avaricious, this-worldly priests.

In this respect the French are akin to the Hindus, among whom the Brahmins, who are their priests, have completely deluded them into believing that a dip in the Ganges will wash away the sins of a lifetime and that rich gifts to Brahmins will open heaven's gate. Hindu scriptures strictly enjoin the giving of alms to Brahmins. A Brahmin may have lakhs of rupees, yet in the hope of getting a rupee or eight annas in charity he will beg from door to door. Clearly, the Brahmins, who are the leaders of Hindu society, enjoined alms-giving as insurance for their descendants who would increase in numbers till some of them in the normal course of events would be poor and helpless, but thanks to this arrangement would be able to live in comfort without toil or labour.

The division of Hindus into castes is an extraordinary thing. The Brahmins are deemed superior to the other castes and it is laid down in their scriptures, the Vedas, that only Brahmins may read them. Anyone else doing so is damned. In all the seventy-two religions mentioned in our books, the followers are enjoined to read their scripture so that they may not be ignorant about the articles of faith, but with the Hindus it is the opposite, and it is nothing but great stupidity. Both the French and the Hindus have such stupid and superstitious customs that they confound wisdom.

The French priests have led their people astray with consummate hypocrisy and have amassed great wealth, but if they were to read the Holy Koran and to believe in Prophet Mohammed as Allah's chosen apostle, there would be little to distinguish their religious practices from those of Islam. Hypocrisy would then form no part of their religion.

Hypocrisy, of course, is not a French monopoly. In India there are hypocrites and intriguers among both Moslems and Hindus. They array themselves as *Fakirs* and *sufis* and enrich themselves with presents from simple-minded devotees. The Firinghees are so disgusted with their corrupt ways that they are blinded to the fact that there are many genuine *Fakirs* and *sufis*, worthy men with firm faith and no hypocrisy. They go so far as to maintain that our saints are incapable of performing miracles, of which, they aver, only their prophets were capable.

Compared to Indians, the English give scant importance to religious observances like prayer, fasting or ritual chanting. Once a week, on

Sunday, men and women congregate in church for prayers. Many of them regard prayer as optional, but others consider it compulsory. They say God created the universe in six days and ordained the seventh day as a day of rest and prayer, when worldly activities must be suspended. This is how these people pray. The men and women in church kneel down with bowed heads. The clergyman reads out passages from the Bible while another group sing hymns to musical accompaniment and punctuate their performance with Amens. French priests round off services with this prayer:

'O Lord, give us our evening meal as you have given us our morning breakfast!' The English object to this because God has allotted food for everyone and so the prayer is redundant. But they believe it is proper to give thanks to God after a meal.

I was told that the French go to church to pray on Wednesday and Sunday. The English by comparison do not attach much importance to prayer. They say God has sent man to this world to enrich and beautify it. In practical terms this means that if we try to build better houses, improve agriculture, invent new machines, add to knowledge, strengthen the realm's defence, find new means of livelihood and find better food and shelter for the myriad creatures in our care, then we are truly fulfilling our divinely ordained role. We must keep an account of our daily activities and plan our activities for the morrow. When on the day of judgement Allah will ask us to provide an account sheet of our activities on earth, those who passed their days in indolence and sleep will be able to show naught and will be punished. If man spends all his time in prayer and grows weak from fasting and chanting on an empty stomach, the activities of the world will be neglected – anarchy will ensue and God's creatures will suffer.

Despite these attitudes the English believe that God is one and has no second. Some among them secretly believe that Christ is the son of God; others exalt reason above the authority of the ancients. Some, like the rationalist 'Mutazila' and naturalist 'Dahriya' schools in Islamic philosophy, do not believe in apocalypse, resurrection, the last judgement, hell or heaven, accounting them to be fictions, and deny that Christ was a prophet or the Torah a revealed book. They say Christ was human as we are and the Torah was composed by Moses. Some go even further and deny that God created the world and the heavens. They claim the earth and the ten heavens have always existed; just as in the case of grass, plants and trees, seeds germinate into new life, which grows, then withers, to be replaced by new growth, similarly men, animals and birds grow, decay and die in a cyclical process.

Allah save us from such misguided ideas.

CHAPTER XII

MORE ON RELIGION

The English say that they would accept Islam if there were any notice of Mohammed's prophetical office in the New Testament. But, they claim, there is no such notice.

The Moslem response to this is as follows. The original books of the New Testament, which were revealed Scriptures, have been lost. After the death of Hazrat Issa four of his apostles – Matthew, Mark, Luke and John – wrote down from memory accounts of his life and teachings, which form the major part of what we now know as the New Testament. So it is impossible to determine whether or not the original book forecast Mohammed's advent.

However, there is no doubt that Hazrat Issa never explicitly prophesied Hazrat Mohammed's advent but only alluded to it metaphorically. Consequently it is not surprising that Christians should doubt Hazrat Mohammed's claim to prophethood.

Hazrat Issa narrates this parable in the New Testament. A rich man who owned a garden went to the bazaar at the first watch of the day and hiring some labourers for one *dirham* per day, sent them to work in the garden. At the second watch he saw another group of labourers standing idle in the bazaar and also hired them for one *dirham* each for the rest of the day. At the third watch he went out again and saw a fresh group of unemployed labourers. When he asked them what they were waiting for they replied, 'We came late and so nobody hired us.' The rich man hired this group as well for one *dirham* for what remained of the day. In the evening the three groups finished work and went to the owner of the garden to be paid and he gave everyone one *dirham*. At this the first group raised a murmur of protest. 'We have worked the whole day,' they said, 'and we have worked hard, and others have worked only during one watch. Yet you have given them the same wage that you have given us.' The master replied: 'Did I not bargain with you to give one *dirham* each?' They said, 'Yes, that is true.' 'Then,' continued the master, 'I have fulfilled my promise to you, and you have no cause for complaint.'

The Moslems consider their position to be akin to that of the third group of labourers. They claim that their prophet was the last to appear on earth, yet he is no less in importance than his predecessors. Consequently they believe that they will enter heaven as the followers of the other prophets – Moses, Jesus, etc. – have before them.

The English say that the holy books were not revealed by God, as people believe, but were written by prophets and apostles. 'The Almighty didn't send them in a written state from Heaven,' they protest. 'You Moslems maintain that Gabriel brought God's word to Mohammed, but who among us has ever seen Gabriel or heard his voice? How can we believe this without proof positive? The truth is that the prophets, who are the spiritual guides of the people, wrote these books according to the best of their knowledge and understanding in order to teach their followers good manners and right conduct. The Torah was written by Moses, the Psalms by David, the New Testament by Christ's apostles and the Koran by Mohammed.'

Though the English do not believe in the Koran and in Prophet Mohammed, they praise his laws. 'Mohammed' they say, 'was unsurpassed for knowledge and wisdom in his age.' But they find a serious fault in him. 'He shed blood,' they complain. 'This is in opposition to the prophetical office and the divine mission. The prophets in the past used admonition and advice to show lost mankind the right path and men became converts willingly. Those who desisted were left alone and those who persecuted the prophets were merely cursed and it was left to God's will to punish them. But no true prophet ever spilt blood.'

Thus did Captain Swinton dispute with me one day. I replied: 'Allah sent many prophets to the world's various nations but their advice and admonitions did not always bring them converts. On the contrary, they were often answered with persecution. This was the experience of Prophet Mohammed as well. He tried favour, kindness, advice, admonitions, gentleness and tendencies, but to no avail. The people were not impressed. Not only that, but soon he and his small following became the victims of tyranny and oppression, especially at the hands of his own tribespeople, the Qureish of Mecca. When their cruelty exceeded the bounds of tolerance and the prophet had lost all hope of bringing them to the path of Islam he begged Allah to tell him what to do. Allah commanded him to make war against the infidels and ever since *jihad* or holy warfare has been a divine obligation among Muslims. Through the prophet's *jihad* Allah avenged himself on the unbelievers. Thus it was at the instance of the Almighty that the prophet spilt blood, and not from his own wishes.

After I returned from Vilayet I gave a similar answer to Mr. John Graham in Burdwan. This sahib was continually arguing about Islam with the two brothers Munshi Mir Sudruddin and Munshi Mir Sirajuddin. He claimed that Mohammed was not a prophet and did not possess miraculous powers and the two Munshis neither did nor could refute him convincingly. One evening at the fag end of such a debate, in which several other sahibs were also present, Mr. Graham was merrily cracking jokes at the expense of our prophet, when I entered and heard him saying, 'Muslims believe they will enter heaven by Mohammed's intercession and everyone else will be sent to hell. This is an unreasonable belief, for Mohammed couldn't perform any miracle like a true prophet. One of the miracles told about him is utterly spurious. He bred a pigeon and set it free in the hills and when he felt the people desired a miracle he climbed a hill and closing his hand showed it to the pigeon, which in expectation of grain came and alighted on his shoulder. Then he addressed the gathered crowd thus: 'Behold. I am Allah's prophet, for the creatures of the wild obey me.' The two Munshis were offended at this affront to our prophet but like men of simple faith they could not reply with anything but an appeal to the authority of the Koran and the *Sunna*, thus: 'Allah declares in the Holy Koran that Hazrat Mohammed, peace be upon him, is the last prophet on earth and the chief intercessor from man on the day of judgement. He caused the sun to turn back, the moon to split in two and trees to walk by themselves. But if these miracles do not inspire faith in the Holy Koran and our traditions we can only quote the common saying: "If anyone will not yield consent to the Koran the answer is this. To him let no answer be given".'

At this Mr. Graham shook his head, laughed and said, 'Since I do not believe in your Koran and other books, how can I be convinced by all you say?' At this juncture I went forward and said. 'If you will allow me I shall say something on this subject.' Everyone turned towards me and I continued, 'I learn from the translation of the New Testament in my possession and from various works of history that the miracles performed by the prophets of the past hardly won them any converts. This is particularly true of Hazrat Issa, who performed more miracles than any other prophet. He brought the dead back to life, restored eyesight to the blind and cured leprosy and other diseases, yet in his lifetime there were few besides the twelve apostles who believed in him. The New Testament says that the Jews went on persecuting him and at last crucified him. Our prophet too performed many miracles but he was still persecuted and in the end, at Allah's command, he was forced to wage war to preserve the faith. All this goes to show that the world has always abounded with wicked and sinful men – in the time of Hazrat Issa, in the time of Hazrat Mohammed and even in our time. If one of these bastards doesn't believe in our prophet there is nothing we can do except wait for Allah to straighten out things on the day of judgement.'

Mr. Graham felt offended and insulted but could say nothing. The two Munshis quickly took leave and taking me by my hands accompanied me home. They were full of praise for me and kept saying that they could never have clinched the argument as I had done. They also eagerly borrowed the translation of the New Testament from me so that they could make copies of it. Since that day Mr. Graham never disputed with Munshis on religious matters.

One day Captain Swinton said to me: 'Moslems believe everything depends on predestination and their own efforts count for nothing. This attitude has its good points, I admit, but our nation puts its faith in wisely applied effort, which it sets above fate. We believe anything can be achieved through proper use of intelligence and discernment – of course mistakes through carelessness will foil our efforts. But you Indians believe that fate alone determines the success of all endeavours, whether great or small. If a china plate or bottle falls from your hand and breaks you say it was predestined.

'Or take a very different example: A certain Duke commanding an army is very brave and well versed in the arts of war. He disciplines and exercises his men, equips them with the best weapons and easily defeats an ill-trained and badly equipped foe even though it is twice as numerous. Your people will say his victory is a gift of Providence, but surely that is an absurdity.'

I replied, 'The divine will is supreme but Allah has also created man superior to other beings and has endowed him with understanding and wisdom. Allah has commanded man to use his faculties in both worldly and spiritual activities, but whether or not success will attend his efforts depends on what has been preordained since before Creation. For example, a farmer may plough his land and sow the seed in accordance with the rules of good husbandry but what avails such efforts if through the predestination of Providence no rain falls? Because fate is the ultimate ruler over everything. But you are right in pointing out that our people are inordinately fatalistic. They sit down with folded arms and let Providence take care of everything. This is wrong, for it is a precondition of intelligence that it should be used.'

Whenever Captain Swinton had guests for dinner they would send for me because they wanted to see me and ask me about my views on religion and social mores. I may add without immodesty that they were always satisfied with my replies. One day General Munro and Captain Ouderman were present along with several others. They said to me: 'You are all alone in this country. Why don't you take a wife?'

I answered: 'It is impossible for me to marry here because of two reasons. The first is that any woman I may wish to marry won't have me. The second is that any woman who might be willing to have me I can't approve of. What I mean is that though I am considered well-born in my country a well-born Englishwoman cannot consider a union with a foreigner of a different religion. Likewise, an Englishwoman of inferior class might be willing to marry me, but I wouldn't have her.'

My audience was vastly amused and burst out laughing.

Next they turned to religion and said to me: 'God first created

Adam and then *Bibi Hawa* [Eve] to be his mate. From this we can say that the principle of monogamy is divinely ordained. Why does your religion violate it, allowing you to take up to four wives? Further, why did your prophet marry nine wives but allow only four to his followers?'

I replied: 'The Almighty created woman to provide ease and comfort to man, and gave Bibi Hawa to Hazrat Adam as wife. But when Adam's descendants increased He commanded that if one wife didn't please a man he might take another. Prophet Mohammed allowed us up to four at one and the same time. Five he forbade; but if one died we might marry another in her stead. There is respectable precedent for his injunction. Hazrat Ibrahim [Abraham] had two wives, Bibi Sara and Bibi Hejira; Hazrat Solomon had one hundred and sixty wives; and Hazrat Dawood [David] went against law and custom to have Uriah's wife. Besides, can you sincerely declare that those who live with only one wife have never committed adultery, either in reality or in their hearts.'

Next they said: 'God in his infinite kindness has made a great gift to his servants by giving them wine, but your prophet has deprived you of it by prohibiting its use.'

I said: 'Wine itself is a good thing but the intoxication it causes is bad, for it makes people lose their wits or even forget God. The Almighty's command in this regard is this: "Eat and drink as you please, but you must not forget me for a minute".'

Then they countered: 'If a person drinks in moderation he will not lose his senses, it will make him feel happy.'

I clinched the argument with this retort: 'Can any of you remember an instance when you drank without becoming intoxicated?'

The guests turned to religion again. 'You believe,' they said, 'that if anyone in his heart should even once sincerely recite the confession of faith in Mohammed – *La ilaha illallah Mohammadur Rusel ullah*: There is no God but Allah and Mohammed is his prophet – he will enter heaven and those who haven't done so will all go to hell. Now the Moslems are few in number: they are to be found only in Turkey, Syria, Persia, Arabia and India. Those of other faiths are more numerous and yet you say they will be damned. Do you mean to say God created his servants only for the purpose of burning them in hell?'

I replied: 'Certainly, for we believe that though Muslims are few in number, heaven was created for them alone. Other people are more numerous; for this reason hell is four times large than paradise.'

I continued. 'Though all men are God's servants, some among them are obedient, some wise, some honest, some are fools, some thieves, and some without probity. Hazrat Issa narrates a parable regarding this in the New Testament. A certain person had three sons. Once, upon setting out on a journey, he decided to test their intelligence and honesty, and for this purpose gave one thousand rupees to each. The eldest son buried his money in the ground, from where a thief carried it off. The second son gave his to a banker and spent the interest on himself. But the third son invested his money and doubled it.

'When the father returned from his journey he asked his sons for the money with which he had entrusted them. The eldest son told his father how his money had been stolen. The second son returned the thousand rupees, whereupon the father said to him, "You are wise by halves," and gave him a small present. The youngest son returned the original thousand rupees as well as the profit he had made. The father rejoiced at this, and said, "You are both wise and honest." He then entrusted the youngest son with the management of his estate.

'Hazrat Issa explained the meaning of the parable in this manner: "Before God it is so ordered that the individual who retains the whole of the original sums will have the whole made over to him; he who has retained less will have less given to him; and he who preserves nothing will be left with empty hands."

'Muslims interpret the parable as follows: The foolish man represents those who are ignorant and disobedient. The sum of money stands for faith; and the thief is the devil, who steals the faith of fools and careless persons, who thereby are deprived of the Almighty's mercy and are cast into hell. The second son, who squandered the interest, represents the hypocrites, who have partial faith in God, but consider God's prophets to be imposters; their place is also hell. The youngest son, who by faith and good work not only presented his father with the original sum but also with a large profit, represents the Muslims, for they attest God to be their nourisher by word and thought. They rely upon God and do not deviate a hair's breadth from his laws and the injunctions of his prophets. They consider the world a perishable place and in the hope of finding a permanent home in heaven they lead a hard and austere life, gladly accepting difficulties and sufferings. They say that in this world are sown the seeds of futurity, after the Arab saying, "The world is the field of futurity." Surely, they will without any doubt see paradise.

'Muslims account worldly wealth useless and do not follow the example of those who take great pains to acquire riches and are rewarded with nothing more than the enjoyment of wealth: the paradise of such people is this earth and they have no hope of entry into heaven.

'In man's estate, grief and gladness are intermingled. After joy comes sorrow, and grief is succeeded by mirth. Sorrow does not always depress, nor does gladness continually prevail. And so Muslims, who condemn wealth and suffer tribulations on account of their faith, will in the end receive truly lasting riches – in heaven – while those who now indulge in worldly pleasure will soon be condemned to everlasting sorrow and grief.'

CHAPTER XIII

THE ENGLISH POLITY

England used to be an insignificant country, in which seven independent kings ruled side by side. Even with the addition of Ireland and Scotland the kingdom is less than twice the size of Bengal.

I learnt that there is a coastal region in France whose inhabitants differ slightly from other Frenchmen in customs and manners. An ambitious and powerful king of this region attacked England with a huge army, conquered the tiny English kingdoms and united them with Ireland in one large empire. This king through his justice and evenhandedness won the hearts of English commoners and noblemen alike. He began to mingle with his English subjects and adopted their customs and manner. The English counted themselves lucky to have such a just and powerful king and pledged their undying loyalty to him. After some years the fortunate King raised a huge army and conquered France. But at the humble entreaties of the French he agreed to a peace and handed back the throne to the French King, but on his return to England he struck French coins in his name. Since then every English monarch has considered himself sovereign over England, France, Holland and Scotland and struck coins accordingly.

For many years now, the descendants of William have ruled over England. Among them has been one named George. The present monarch is George III; he is nearly sixty years old now. The real cause of the enmity between France and England is the English monarch's claim of sovereignty over France. The French have an overpowering desire to defeat the English and wipe off the ignominy of having the royal seal of England on their coins. After that they can make an honourable peace. But till now, i.e. 1780 AD, their desire has not been fulfilled. What the future holds Allah alone knows.

King George III, who now occupies the throne of England, is praised as a wise and brave monarch. When this writer saw him he was a well-built and good-looking man in his fifties. His queen too was comely, albeit of slender physique. She is the Danish King's sister. The custom of the English royal family is to marry into other European royal houses. As a result of the union relations between England and Denmark are very cordial. When I was in England the royal couple had twelve children; I hear the number has since increased to nineteen.

The country is administered with such fairness and justice that it is united in its loyalty to the Crown, to which there is no opposition at all. If the King is wise and just and if there is not discord between him and the princes and aristocracy, he will be able to command absolute obedience from his subjects, who will also under such a dispensation be united and disciplined. But if the king is a tyrant in whom the subjects can't repose trust, there will be dissension among the royal officials, and no matter how rich the kingdom, it will go into decline; dark days will engulf it; the subjects will suffer; there will be anarchy all round. Present-day India is a perfect example.

In matters of government the King of England is not independent like the Great Moghul of India. In all state affairs he can do nothing without first consulting his ministers and nobles, and a few men selected from the middle classes. If, as has happened in India, there is discord among the ruling classes, wealth and the reins of government will leave their hands, as this verse succinctly proclaims:

Concord conduces to wealth,
Discord begets poverty,
Many Kings who heeded not their ministers
Have lost both dignity and sovereignty.

There are four departments in charge of running the administration. The first is the Judiciary, which is responsible for trying all cases of law. The second is the bureaucracy, responsible for collecting taxes, keeping accounts, looking after the state treasury, running the various government offices and supervising state expenditures. The third is a body of loyal advisors comprising members of the nobility, and the fourth is the body of military commanders who are entrusted with the country's defence, the upkeep of garrisons, the army, and the navy and its battleships. In all administrative and fiscal matters these four departments have full powers. If war has to be declared or peace made it is the third department whose recommendations are paramount; all the king can do is issue a royal proclamation accordingly. The people even have power to appoint or depose a king or, if necessary, reduce his powers. They say, 'The King is the protector of the subjects, appointed to be the country's guardian. If he takes care of us we will obey him, but if he is tyrannical, selfish, ignorant, insensible or immoral, our duty is to replace him.' In such an event someone else is chosen from the royal family or from the aristocracy for his wisdom, courage and greatness and placed on the throne and everyone then pledges allegiance to him. If his royal decrees and proclamations are just and lawful and according to the wishes of his subjects, they are followed to the letter. But if the king's commands go against the interests of the citizens then even the humblest of them will say straight to his face. 'Sir, I do not recognise your authority.'

Following the king's death his eldest son is placed on the throne if he is capable of holding the reins of the kingdom. Otherwise he who is deemed most worthy among the younger sons is chosen. If the king dies childless either a prince of an older royal family or a prominent nobleman is chosen king and administered the oath of office in Church. The day of the coronation is celebrated throughout the kingdom by rich and poor alike. But if this king ever becomes drunk with power and forgetting his oath begins to tyrannise his subjects the prominent citizens with popular support will move to dethrone him and replace him with someone more able and just. Under such conditions the king cannot but behave justly and with consideration towards all subjects; consequently there is little chance of indiscipline and anarchy. For these reasons, compared to other countries the signs of stability, glory and progress are more conspicuous here. Specialists in jurisprudence opine that the English system of government is the best in the world. They point out that wherever monarchs can rule arbitrarily, the subjects suffer and the state eventually faces collapse. Even if the monarch of such a kingdom is a just and able administrator he may be succeeded by a son who is the opposite and who rules with the help of some court officials. If his brothers are at variance with him there will be a bloody war of succession. For this reason whoever can capture the throne after a king's death will put his rivals to death or imprison them. Sometimes the fear of usurpation drives a father to murder his sons, or a son to murder his father.

A cunning and treacherous minister can reduce a monarch to ineffectuality and rule as the grey eminence. He can then depose a King and install another as he pleases, or even blind a King and keep him confined. The experiences of the unfortunate Gaziuddin Khan, Ahmed Shah, Badshah Alamgir II and the present Badshah Shah Alam will bear out my point. In England on the other hand, where all laws are passed with the consent of the people, there is no room for such developments. The excellence of the English political system is that even if the ministers make such mistakes as all human beings are prone to, the polity is not damaged beyond repair. Of course in politics as in all matters the will of Allah is paramount. Still, man's duty is to try to ensure that the prime prerequisites of a sound body politic, viz. unity, foresight and caution are not ignored.

In England everyone is free; no one can lord it over another, and there is no such thing as master and slave: which is totally different from other countries in which all are slaves of the King. In England both great and small would be greatly ashamed at the term 'slave'. They say, 'We call one person King, for, without that, government could not be carried on, and therefore we have set a ruler over us; but we all individually take some charge in governing. Our nation, in order to increase its renown in conflicts with our enemies, sacrifices both life and estate, but no one is a slave. However, we do not deviate a hair's breadth in paying due respect and honour to the King and his ministers; and in the same way, his Majesty thinks it incumbent on him to show a proper regard for his subjects, and rules in a mild and gentle manner.'

At a royal durbar the King stands with crowned head while his courtiers come up one by one to make obeisance with bare head and on bent knee. When this is over, he climbs a gem-studded throne, and his brothers and sons take their seats to his right and left, on a lower level. Further away and in order of rank are seated the emirs, lords, generals and colonels. If the King deems it necessary to wage war against any country he summons a *majlis* [meeting] of notables and standing bareheaded before it, makes an appeal: 'We are faced with a crisis. If you rise to meet it you will help preserve our sovereignty and add to the nation's glory.' The assembly rises as one man, makes obeisance, and replies: 'We owe you full obedience and we are ready for any sacrifice to defeat the enemy.' But were the King to order arrogantly, 'Go and fight,' the assembly would curtly reply, 'We are not your slaves. Go and fight yourself.'

The Armed Forces:

The officers in the Army and Navy are organised in hierarchical ranks, viz. Sergeant, Ensign, Lieutenant, Captain, Major, Colonel, Lord, Duke and finally the King himself. Each unit has three officers, so that if the Commanding Officer is killed or incapacitated the officer next in seniority may take over command. To English soldiers their commanders' orders are like divine injunctions and are obeyed to the letter; the slightest deviation is an unpardonable and punishable offence.

In the many cantonments scattered throughout the country the soldiers – both foot and cavalry – are engaged solely in military exercises in accordance with the instructions of their commanders; these include horsemanship, weapon training, musketry and gunnery. The commanders, like their Indian counterparts, are devoted primarily to carrying out the orders of the King and his government. To each commander is attached a squad of runners, varying in strength from one to twelve, according to the commander's rank, whose task is to carry orders and messages between him and his troops. A troop of fifty horsemen and foot soldiers are detailed to guard the King's palace and wait upon him.

In peace time the officers generally live at home, where they can attend to private business, but at the first sign of war they rush to their stations and prepare for battle. Every Sunday they report to the royal court to collect their salaries. They are forbidden to make private visits abroad, for if there is a sudden outbreak of war they will be required to report for duty within a day or two. Anyone who neglects his duties in such emergencies is at once arrested and punished; even the intercession of high-ranking officers will avail him naught.

The soldiers in the Royal Army – both dragoons and foot – are carefully selected and trained. They must be robust and of proper height. They are fitted out in clean clothes of one colour and instructed in drill and martial exercises. A cavalry regiment consists of seven hundred horses, and is distinguished by a colour: thus one regiment is black, another white or bay. For this reason a number of regiments exercising in consort present a splendid sight. I had the opportunity to see such exercises twice – first in London, then in Scotland. The soldiers receive rations and uniforms from the government, in addition to a pay of eight rupees a month.

I was told that in the first war with France, the English forces comprised one and a half lakh foot soldiers and cavalrymen, and sailors and marines. When I was in Vilayet, the country had one hundred and fifty warships of different sizes ready for war; one, named after the King, carried one hundred and sixty guns, and another, named after the Queen, one hundred and fifty. These two ships are particularly renowned, for none of the ships in other European navies can match them. The English give special importance to the construction of large and sturdy warships, and excel all other European nations in naval warfare; they have a natural genius for it. I hear that at present they have five hundred warships in full preparedness; their navy is so large and their army so well-equipped that none of the other Firinghee nations can ever hope to conquer them. They say England is an island fortress. In times of war her numerous warships are fully equipped and patrol her waters. In peace time many of them are unrigged and have their masts struck as they lie in well-protected harbours; but at the first sign of war they are quickly fitted out and sent to sea.

The English are celebrated throughout the world for bravery and skill in military tactics. Many of their military regulations differ materially from those of other countries. One is that deviation from an officer's orders by even a hair's breadth is punished either by death or by dishonourable discharge, after which the offender is unable to serve again. Another is that flight from battle is an unpardonable offence, whose punishment is death, even if the offender is an old officer, an aristocrat, or a prince. Retreat is a capital offence even if the enemy is twice as numerous, and even then it is to be resorted to when unavoidable and according to cautious tactical procedure, so that the troops don't lose discipline or morale. The aim of such retreat is to fight one's way, with as little loss as possible, to a tactically more advantageous position. If even such retreat is impossible and a force is totally surrounded by vastly superior numbers, the soldiers are expected to die fighting like heroes. Victory over numerically superior forces is rewarded with promotions and decorations.

According to another military regulation, all plunder, though it amount to lakhs and crores of rupees, is to be distributed amongst the men and officers according to rank. This is contrary to the custom of other nations, in Europe and elsewhere. The French and Portuguese, for instance, give a quarter of the booty to the soldiers and the rest goes to the royal treasury. The motive of the English in giving away the whole of the booty is to give the troops incentive to be more valiant. This policy works very well in keeping officers and men in fine fettle.

The English avoid self-praise and even consider it disgraceful to talk of their own exploits. If an officer who has distinguished himself for courage and enterprise in an expedition is asked about his experiences he will simply state the bare facts. If another person greatly extols him in his presence, he at once casts his eyes on his feet and remains silent, and from extreme bashfulness the perspiration distils from his face. The English in general not only do not relish being praised before their face, but are annoyed at it. They think egotists are essentially cowards; and sycophants and flatterers, liars. Consequently it is unusual to hear flattery among them.

Sensible people everywhere despise egotists and flatterers; yet, the sepoys and officers in India, particularly in Delhi, think that egotism and flattery add to their consequence. Thus if a person with great difficulty succeeds in killing a fox, he will go about loudly proclaiming that he has killed a lion. He twirls his moustache in a most valiant manner and swells with pride till it seems his clothes will burst at the seams. He dismisses the deeds of others as nothing in comparison to his own, and even makes out Rustum [legendary Persian hero] to have been decrepit.

Revenue Matters:
Unlike Bengal, tax and revenue collectors in England do not resort to extortion. That the zemindars of Bengal now have no worries about the payment of land revenue is due to the introduction of the English system of tax collection by the East India Company. Instead of waiting for a summons or a visit from the bailiff, English tenants go voluntarily to the landlord and pay their annual rent in two instalments. The rent that the landlord receives from each tenant and also the revenue that he in turn pays to the government are fixed. Any attempt to extort more than the fixed rent will provoke a tenants' revolt. In times of famine or crop failure, a portion of the rent is excused. During war, on the other hand, the rent and revenue are doubled; but the old rates are restored with peace.

Compared to India, the land area of Vilayet is very little. Also, the revenue from the land is much less than the taxes from trade and other sources. The taxes on householders are levied according to the number of doors, windows, rooms, floors, balconies, etc. in their houses, and the number of carriages they own. This principle is not followed in any other country. Besides, separate taxes are levied to pay for the building and repair of roads.

When war breaks out at least twenty-five crore rupees must be raised in taxes to pay for the cost. Only fifty lakhs come from land revenue; the rest come from other taxes. War seems to be an expensive business with the English. The total cost for the recent American war and the wars with France, Spain and other countries amounts to one hundred and twenty nine crore, seventy lakh, eighteen thousand, seven hundred and seven rupees, of which all but two and a half crore came from the government treasury.

The Judiciary:
In the English judicial system, which has lately been introduced into Bengal, when a dispute arises, whether over a civil or a criminal matter, both plaintiff and defendant appear in court with professional advocates to argue their cases. It may take the court months or even years to give judgement, in which case both parties have to spend immense sums in lawyers' and court fees. The losing side has to pay the expenses of the other.

A strict code of conduct is enjoined. Neither bribes nor gifts are permitted; if one party attempts bribery, even if its cause is just, the judges will assume otherwise. No partiality is shown to people of rank. If a prince or nobleman rides through another's field, damaging the crop, and the farmer brings a complaint, the offender is ordered to compensate the loss ten times over and also pay a fine to the court. This law is designed to deter the rich and powerful from oppressing the poor and weak.

The English law regarding murder is very different from the Islamic, according to which a killer may obtain pardon from the victim's kinsmen, or, failing that, from the judges on payment of a fine. In England, if the judges find that a life has been wilfully taken, the criminal is sentenced to death. But the judgement must be the result of mature deliberation; besides, the procedure of the trial is such as to preclude the easy assumption of culpability. Thus, if the indicted person confesses to the crime under interrogation, his word is not automatically accepted, but on the supposition that he might be temporarily deranged and hence an unreliable witness, he is merely incarcerated. But if on two subsequent occasions he repeats his confession, it is taken to establish his guilt, and he is sentenced to be executed. On the other hand, if the indicted person is in full command of his wits and denies the charge, it is up to the prosecuting counsel to prove his guilt by presenting evidence, witnesses and clever arguments. The defence counsel meanwhile tries to undermine the evidence of prosecution witnesses by raising many ifs and buts. This may annoy the plaintiff so much that he goes absent; if he stays away for a whole day, the court dismisses the case and releases the defendant.

English law also differs from Muslim law in the punishment of theft. Whereas Muslim law orders that the thief should have a hand cut off if more than eight annas' worth is stolen, English law prescribes the death penalty for all thieves. The English argue that it is not the value of what is stolen that should determine the punishment, but the criminal's intention. A thief will take as much as he can lay his hands on; therefore his punishment should be irrespective of what he actually succeeds in stealing, and in all cases of theft it is death. But in spite of this England abounds with pickpockets, burglars and robbers.

European gentlemen, whenever they go out, carry money, in the form of gold, silver and banknotes, and a watch, in their pockets.

And as they are in the habit of frequenting crowded places like bazaars, pleasure gardens and theatres, they become the quarry of cut-purses and pickpockets who at the slightest opportunity cut open people's pockets and speedily transfer the contents into their own. If, however, the thief is caught red-handed, he is hanged.

There are many mounted robbers, or highwaymen, in England who prey on travellers on the highways. Some of them are sons of wealthy parents who have squandered their patrimony in gaming and debauchery and then taken to a life of crime. They lie in wait in places removed from human habitation, like forests or open commons, and at the approach of a carriage gallop up to it and clapping a pistol to the head of the traveller, orders him to deliver whatever he has got if he wishes to escape alive. The poor fellow has no choice but to hand over his money, gold and other valuables. However, I heard two stories of the table being turned on the highwaymen.

A certain great man who was travelling in a carriage observed a horseman approaching him with the speed of an arrow. He knew at once that it was a highwayman, and he quickly loaded a pistol and put it in his pocket. The highwayman came up, pistol in hand, and commanded, 'Surrender what you've got.' The gentleman took the pistol out of his pocket, and saying, 'Take this!', he shot the robber through the heart.

In the other incident, a man who had been robbed of bank-notes and valuables went to the Bank as soon as he arrived in town and reported the crime and gave a description of the notes, so that when the highwayman went there to get change he was immediately arrested and, after trial, executed. The banknotes were returned to the owner.

If a woman complains that she has been raped and the charge is proved in court, the offender is at once sentenced to be hanged. But English courts have nothing to do with simple cases of fornication. Where there is mutual consent a man and a woman may fornicate without fear of the *kotwal* [Police Superintendent]; as the saying goes in that country, what business has the Superintendent in another's bedroom? Unlike India, the *kotwal* has no power in England to seize a fornicator or a fornicatress. Nonetheless there is a stigma attached to fornication in polite society. If a lady of position is discovered to be a fornicatress, other gentlewomen will roundly condemn her and make an outcaste of her. In a case of adultery, if the injured husband catches his wife in flagrante delicti he is within his rights to kill her and her lover. But if it so happens that he has no weapon on him and goes to fetch one, and meanwhile the lovers separate and deny having been together, the injured husband cannot kill the offenders with impunity; if he does he will be tried as a murderer and sentenced to death. If a husband brings a charge of adultery against his wife, the court will not accept the case if he cannot produce at least three credible witnesses.

A French priest once presented a translation of the New Testament to the Emperor Akbar, in which there was the following narrative. Certain Jewish doctors brought an adulteress before Hazrat Issa, with the intention of playing a trick on him. They had thought up a question for him, a negative reply to which would amount to condoning a sin, while an affirmative reply would be tantamount to cruelty. That is to say, if the prophet ordered the woman to be stoned, they would protest that it contradicted his philosophy of universal mercy, pity and love, and if he pardoned her they would accuse him of ignoring the divinely ordained distinction between right and wrong. Reasoning thus among themselves, the Jews asked Hazrat Issa if he would abide by the Mosaic law and condemn the adulteress to be stoned to death. The prophet replied, 'Let he who is without sin among you cast the first stone.' Then he bowed his head and began writing in the dust with his finger. The men gathered around him gazed at the writing and by God's will and the prophet's spiritual powers each saw inscribed therein an accurate description of his lifetime's sins. In shame and remorse, the men filed out of the room leaving the woman and the prophet alone. Then Hazrat Issa asked the woman, 'Where have the men gone?' She replied, 'They left one by one without saying anything about me.' The prophet then said, 'I too shall say nothing to you, except this – repent and don't commit this sin again.'

However, in the translation of the Bible that I brought from Vilayet, this story is not narrated in exactly this form. Captain Swinton opined that the Portuguese priests who went as ambassadors to Emperor Akbar's court altered it.

The moral standpoint of Hazrat Mohammed (Peace be upon him) on the question of adultery and fornication is revealed in another story. One day, when the Prophet was seated with some of his companions, a woman came before him and confessed that she was a fornicatress and begged that the punishment prescribed by law be meted to her, so that she might be spared on the Day of Judgement. The Prophet looked away, pretending not to hear, but when she persisted with her plea, he turned towards her and, noticing that she was pregnant, said that her punishment was deferred till she was delivered of the child.

After the child was born the woman came back, carrying it in her arms, and repeated her plea. The Prophet replied that as the child was newborn the punishment was remitted till it was weaned. But when the weaning was completed the Prophet objected that as the child was devoid of understanding punishment had to be postponed till it was seven years old.

When the woman returned again the Prophet declared, 'Your child is still young and unwise. Until it attains puberty you cannot be punished, for none will be as kind and protective to a child as its parents, nor will anyone else accept the responsibility to rear and educate it.'

At this one of his companions said, 'O Prophet, since this woman comes time after time to trouble you, I will take charge of the child and rear and educate it, and let her petition be granted.'

The Prophet grew red with anger on hearing this, and turning to his companion he said, 'Who told you to offer your services? Can't you guess that I've always been trying to find pretexts to put off the mother's punishment?'

The Companion was greatly ashamed at this.

Such was the compassion of the Prophet Mohammed.

The East India Company:
A company is a group of persons organised with a common purpose. In common parlance it is a group of businessmen or traders who pool their capital and conduct their business as partners. There are many companies in England, all paying tribute to the King, and the one involved in business in India, China and other countries of the Orient is the East India Company. (Similarly other companies are named after the regions in which they trade.) Its proprietors number over two thousand, but its management is in the hands of twenty-four directors. They are collectively responsible for the government

of the company's territories, for examining its records and accounts and for its administration and activities. For this they receive fat salaries and a share of profits. But for all this they are still of the merchant class and therefore inferior in rank and status to the emirs of the land, the King's ministers, or the landed gentry. By the same token if a captain of his Majesty's forces comes to India he accounts himself superior to a colonel in the Company's army.

Before a ship carrying the Company's employees to India is due to leave royal officials take down the particulars of all on board and pass them on to their superiors for examination and approval, without which the ship is not allowed to set sail. This is done to ensure that neither criminals nor anyone in excess of the number that the Company has been permitted to recruit can leave the country.

When ships arrive in England from the East, the Company's cargoes are exempted from duties, but the personal effects of passengers are thoroughly searched for Bengal muslin, silks, opium and other items that are scarce in Europe and enjoy a cachet as gifts. A private citizen is not allowed to bring these into the country, even for personal use, without first paying a heavy duty. Even a nobleman will be fined five hundred rupees and have his effects seized if a silk handkerchief, a *tola* of opium or a piece of silk is found in his trunk.

I have already mentioned the scrape with Customs when our packet boat reached Dover, but I haven't told the whole story. I had a number of handkerchiefs in my trunk and, as I have already stated, Mrs. Peacock had bolts of kincob and flowered cotton. For this reason the packet, together with the belongings of the Peacocks, Captain Swinton and myself, were detained at the Customs house for fifteen days and, even after we arrived in London, our effects were not released for a month. The matter underwent an investigation in a court of law, in the course of which it came out that a Customs officer, who had once been a soldier, had got drunk and tried to violate Mrs. Peacock's chastity. As compensation for this insult, the belongings of the Peacock's were released with fines. As for my handkerchiefs, the gentlemen of the court said, 'This is but a trifle. The handkerchiefs were not brought for sale, and besides, the Munshi being an Indian visiting England for the first time, is not acquainted with our laws and customs. We therefore pardon his offence.'

When the Company needs military assistance they petition the

King, and if the petition is granted, after due examination by his minister, the required forces are allotted. Their upkeep and wages are henceforth the Company's responsibility. If a soldier falls ill or is wounded while serving the Company, he is fed and clothed as usual and given medical care till he is fit to resume duty. If any citizen of Vilayet dies abroad for want of care, the Company's local agent will be punished and fined. For the protection of the Company's fleet against Turkish, habshi and other pirates, seven or eight battle-ready warships are allotted under an Admiral's command. Other hat-wearing Firinghee nations also assist their companies in similar ways.

English law prescribes that each year the citizens of a town will elect an administrator who is outstanding for honesty, wisdom and public-spiritedness. He is paid a fat salary and is comparable in status to a Calcutta zemindar; he bears the title of Lord Mayor. On the day of his investiture people of all ages and classes from the town and its environs gather and, in a procession, accompany the Mayor, who is fitted out in ceremonial robes, to the town hall and the church, where he takes an oath to fulfil his duties with honesty and justice. After this there is a feast in which as many as ten thousand people eat and drink to their hearts' content. A lottery is held, for which a ticket costs twenty or so rupees. The prize money therefore amounts to two lakh rupees, which is enough to make the winner a wealthy man. Once a shoemaker won two lakh rupees in the lottery, and there are others of such humble background whom the lottery has made rich. The truth is that national wellbeing and peoples' welfare is a product of national unity; indeed, it is impossible to think of any disadvantages accruing from unity.

Besides the Lord Mayor a number of other persons are also elected to a town's administrative council, as we saw in Calcutta in Warren Hastings' time.

CHAPTER XIV

EDUCATION AND CODE OF LIFE

The upper classes in England educate their children in a way totally different from that of the people of India, where the teacher is retained as a servant in the house so that there is little chance that the child will be a victim of the evil eye, or be possessed by evil spirits or fall ill far from home. In England it is usual for people of rank, be they emirs or ministers, to send their children to distant places of education and entrust their care to the teachers. The annual expenses are paid in advance, covering board and lodging, tuition, and also money for clothes, medical expenses, barbers, etc. English schools do not employ barbers on their premises, so students have to go out for a haircut. Those whose families live nearby can visit them on Sunday, otherwise it's no oftener than at the end of a month or a year.

Boys and girls, on average, are kept in school till their twentieth year. The method of education is as follows: First of all the child is taught the letters of the alphabet, which are written on the board; this prepares them for learning the proper spelling of words. Next come the parts of speech, together with which they are set exercises in sentence construction. Then for two years they are given pleasant tales to read, whereby they become adept at the art of reading. This is followed by lessons in arithmetic. After they have mastered reading, writing and arithmetic they are instructed in law, religion, the natural sciences, anatomy, physiology and medicine, and various other disciplines. The pedagogues and savants of England have written books on difficult subjects in such a simple manner that even the beginner has no difficulty in acquiring knowledge. The invention of printing has made books so abundant that if one wishes to buy

10,000 copies of books on each of the various disciplines he will be able to do so from a single bookshop. Besides, books are also very cheap; while a copy of the *Shah Namah* will cost several hundred rupees in India, here it is obtainable for ten or twelve.

Affluent Englishmen begin the education of their children as soon as they reach four years of age. Henceforth the child is never permitted to be idle but must constantly employ himself in reading, writing and the study of the various arts and sciences. Among the English, if a man or woman is unacquainted with music, or is unable to dance or ride, he will not find a place in society. Indeed, people of substance will judge him to be of mean parentage and will taunt him. They will say, 'His parents were too poor to pay for his education, and so he is ignorant of everything.' Women who can neither sing nor dance are seen in a very inferior light and they will never make a good match.

All in all, therefore, the system of general education is totally different from that of India, where there are *madrassahs* endowed by the Badshah, emirs or some wealthy citizens. The children of the ordinary people who go to study there have to bear great hardship and humiliation to obtain board and lodging (usually as tutor to the children of the wealthy). The wealthy and aristocratic citizens of course consider it beneath their dignity to send their children to these institutions.

Indians reproach Europeans as being hardhearted to their children, because they send them away to school, but a little thought will prove that this is actually the greatest kindness, since it ensures that the children will become educated and accomplished in the arts and as a result lead richer lives. The manner in which affluent Indians show kindness to their scions only causes them harm. By keeping them home they bring them up in ignorance and consequently they lead vicious and depraved lives when they grow up.

The poor people of England send their children to town schools where the fee for each student is a rupee a week. There are separate schools for girls. The mode of teaching in these schools, as the writer saw for himself, is as follows. The students sit on a form in one line and recite their lessons. The teacher, with a leather strap in his hand, walks down the line. If he notices any mistake in a student's reading he lashes at him with the strap with such force that the student's back and arms become bloody. This may appear to be cruelty but it is nevertheless true that 'The teacher's tyranny is better than the father's love.'

Even among the lower orders all men and women know reading, writing and arithmetic and the fundamentals of a trade, with the exception of the feeble-minded and those whose parents are too poor to send them to school. After their basic schooling the children of poor parents are put to different trades. Europeans are free to learn any trade of their choice. Thus if a man has four sons it won't be surprising if the eldest is a goldsmith, the second a carpenter, the third a shoemaker, the fourth a smith; none among them will suffer any shame on account of his profession. This is the opposite of the situation in India, where the caste system of the Hindus lays down hereditary professions for the different castes. This is so rigid that one can't even sit to dinner with a person of a different caste, far less adopt his profession, which will result in a loss of caste. In England if a man's father happens to have followed a mean employment, the son will not necessarily follow his footsteps but may become a soldier or something else.

There are many business houses or companies in England set up by three or four partners, who employ a number of workers and profitably manufacture and market various useful articles. Those without any means, however, apprentice their children to factories where they learn the necessary skills while working under supervision and are provided food and clothes by their masters. This lasts till they are ten to fifteen years old, by which time they have learned enough to become paid workers. Finally, when they have become fully skilled in their jobs they are given full pay; at this time, if they wish they may leave and look for employment elsewhere or set up a shop or factory on their own. When they have saved some money they can marry, leave their parents' home and set up house independently.

From what I could gather it seemed most of the poorer inhabitants of England lived in this manner. Those who have come to India as footmen or other low-grade officials are Englishmen of the poorer classes. Many of them would find no place in England because they lack any skill. Some of them are quite stupid and illiterate, and many of them are farm labourers who fled to the cities to avoid punishment for crimes and took ship to India as sailors or porters.

Both in France and England I saw a number of orphanages housed in large buildings built at government expense. Here orphans of both sexes are fed, housed and given an education. People from the city and its environs who because of poverty can't care for their children take them to the orphanage officials. It often happens that a prostitute or fornicatrix becomes pregnant and is forced to bear the child because she dare not risk an abortion which is considered a grave sin and is also a capital offence (even the bleeding caused by an abortion, if reported to the Court, is enough to bring down the death penalty.) After the birth of the child such a woman will hide in shame till night, then steal forth with the newborn and deposit it at the orphanage gate. There are thousands of such abandoned children in the orphanages. The government employs numerous persons to bring up and educate the orphans: each orphanage has a principal, guards, physicians, maids, matrons, male servants and teachers of various trades. They take the forsaken creatures into their arms with motherly affection and give them what they need – food, clothing, swings, beds, etc. As soon as they are able the children are taught to read and write. Thus they are instructed in different trades. There are separate facilities for educating the girls after they have learnt to read and write because they are taught feminine trades, like sewing. The boys are trained in everything from tailoring and the blacksmith's trade to soldiering and shipbuilding. In one orphanage I visited I saw a replica of a ship in the middle of the yards, complete with all the accoutrements of a ship. On it the boys practised how to raise and lower sails, etc. When they grow into youths these boys will enlist in the King's Army or Navy, or perhaps the Merchant Navy. When they grow old and can't serve there any more, they can seek employment as policemen or lighters of street lamps.

Though the English reflect little on the afterworld, such is their way of life and social system that they have much to teach us about this life. First of all, there is hardly a single adult in their country who is idle, averse to work, or unwilling to study or to work. Though the English love to indulge themselves, and possess the wherewithal to lead an idle existence, they feel proud to be engaged in a profession and consider it shameful to accept charity. Having given material considerations priority over spiritual ones, the English have devised such rules and procedures for making all endeavours simple and orderly that people cannot but devote themselves to the pursuit of worldly success. From youth till old age their time is spent in study, thoughts of earning a livelihood, and in increasing their wealth. Worldly success attends knowledge of the arts and sciences. Even if there is someone who is indifferent to the acquisition of knowledge, or despite his having the intelligence and means, wilfully avoids taking up any occupation and like Indian youths spends day and night in the pursuit of pleasure or divides his time between feasting and sleeping, the guardians of the law advise him to mind his ways, and if this produces no result, point out the right path with the help of the rod. Even if someone inherits much wealth from his father he doesn't regard the moiety as his own and doesn't spend it for his everyday needs; he sets it apart as savings. He will never spend his inherited capital, and will run his household on his own earnings.

Another custom among these people is to hold in abeyance the divine ordinance relating to the division of an inheritance. This is done in the interest of the country's economic wellbeing, which depends on the prosperity of individual landowners and merchants. If on their deaths their estates are parcelled out among their heirs, the process over a few generations will reduce their size to uneconomic levels, cause general poverty and disaffection and disrupt the country's stability. For this reason the practice here is that the father leaves his estate to his eldest son and only some amount of money to his other children. Even if he dies without doing so, the eldest son inherits all his property and takes it upon himself to provide for the education and other wants of his brothers and sisters till they come of age and for the dowries and other wedding expenses of his sisters. On completing their education the younger brothers enter the professions or trade and try to save enough to buy houses and estates of their own. If, however, a younger brother turns out to be a black sheep and refuses to use his talents to make a living the eldest brother is obliged to support him. But there is such a stigma attached to indolence among all classes in the country that the number of those who are wilfully unemployed is negligible. The social pressure on the individual to be self-reliant is not so high in any other country. Consequently the younger brothers on coming of age without the protective presence of their father are no longer satisfied with merely existing, but are driven by a sense of self-respect to seek their fortunes in the wide world. They struggle to earn as much as they can so that at forty they can return home to buy their own estates, marry well and lead a life of leisure. They strive to give fine clothes, jewellery and carriages to their wives so that their eldest brothers' wife is put in the shade. If a younger brother feels his fortune is too small to enable him to support a wife in such style that she won't feel embarrassed to mix with his sister-in-law, he won't marry at all, but will remain a lifelong bachelor.

My impression of the customs and mores of the Firinghees is that they are such as to conduce to the growth of many great houses and estates out of one. Needless to add, this is possible only out of divine mercy, as may be proved from the fact that all Firinghees have large families, with twenty to twenty-five children. Those who consider their families small will have at least sixteen to nineteen children, and even a really small family will have at least seven or eight. Moreover, nearly all the children live to be adults. Childlessness is rare, almost nonexistent. When Allah's blessing brings about a nation's prosperity, at the root of the prosperity is a rapid increase in population, which cannot occur without His sanction.

The wise men of Vilayet say that the acquisition of worldly wealth is necessary to make life pleasant and easy, while education increases one's knowledge and wisdom and enables one to show the right path to those who seek advice. Worldly riches ought not to be squandered on luxurious living, on fine clothes, choice cuisine and drinks, and on collecting a bevy of singing and dancing women with whom to spend endless days and nights, as the wealthy noblemen of India are wont to do. These Indians shut themselves up with their women in the zenana and become effeminate in their ways, flirting as if they were women. They wear *churidar* trousers and *churidar* turbans, bright kurtas that end in a flared skirt such as women wear, apply perfume to the breast, antimony on their eyes, henna on their palms, stain their teeth with *missee*, and keep long hair, which they groom with scented oils and tie into a knot. And yet, when they go out they make great pomp and display, with many horses and carriages, a numerous retinue, and such loud fanfare that people might take them for heroes returning from battle. There is a mighty roll of drums, rockets go off, standards flutter in the breeze, *nukeebs* [ushers] proclaim their masters' grandiloquent titles in stentorian tones, *chobdars* [mace-bearers] and attendants of all sorts order common subjects out of the way and loudly recite their prayers for the long life and prosperity of their master.

In Vilayet, both the effeminacy and the pomp of ceremony would be mocked and laughed at. In sum, till forty the English apply themselves to business and also travel, and study the wonders and curiosities of the world. Then they return home with their amassed wealth, marry, and live in pleasant retirement with their families.

By contrast, the behaviour of Indians fill me with shame and sorrow. Indian parents arrange marriages for their sons when they are still mere boys; otherwise the sons themselves will be eager to marry as soon as they reach adolescence. If the parents aren't affluent enough to pay for their children's wedding expenses, they will borrow and get into lifelong debt, or beg from relatives and friends. These people regard marriage as a duty of the utmost urgency before which all other activities are insignificant. If the boy has no means of livelihood, no sooner is he married than he is obliged to leave his wife to seek employment in far-flung places, and it may be years before he can return to her. The sorrows of separation in the wife's heart may be easily imagined. In this state it is not unusual for her to bring disgrace and shame on her husband by having illicit liaisons. This state of affairs must be age-old, for the ancient literature in Persian as well as in Hindi, Brij and Bengali, is replete with poems expressing women's grief at being separated from their husbands. The English consider such separation to be very cruel on the wife and contemn it from legal as well as religions points of view. Surely, the English attitude in this regard is the just one.

After they have saved enough to see themselves comfortably through the rest of their lives, which may be till the age of seventy or even eighty, the English do not give themselves up to indolence, but spend their time in studious and creative pursuits. They engage in researches in science, medicine and technology, make scholarly studies in fields like history and philosophy, seek means to improve the efficiency of factories and machinery, and write books so that mankind may benefit from their discoveries. How different they are from the Indian gentry who are engrossed in writing poems in Persian and Hindi in praise of a mistress' face, or of the wine, the goblet, or a bawd. They pretend to be in love and sigh with lovesickness; in the throes of their bogus passion they become insomniac and turn night into day and day into night. When they essay into Persian prose they adopt a flowery style laden with similes and other figures of speech, obscure idioms and words dredged from dictionaries, forced wordplay, and unfamiliar turns of expression, with the result that the reader's understanding is unnecessarily taxed and wearied. Europeans laugh at this kind of poetry and prose as being useless and futile labour, and dismiss their authors as madmen.

It is common practice among Englishmen to keep their money in banks at an interest, which is paid monthly. They can spend the interest while the principal remains intact. If they wish to enter into business they usually do so in partnership, which increases their chances of success. When they have to transport merchandise they will not put all in one ship, lest they lose all in a shipwreck; but they will divide it among several ships and entrust each consignment in the care of an employee.

Englishmen are so wary of extravagance that even wealthy households are likely to have not more than four servants: a valet, who shaves and dresses the master; a female cook; a chambermaid; and a simple groom for the horses. The master, when he is not attending to the running of his estate, goes on excursions or out hunting. His wife is in overall charge of his household, keeping the accounts and supervising the housework. Many affluent families do not keep a carriage, but hire one when needed. When people of the eminence of lords and ministers go out in a carriage, they have two liveried footmen standing at the back of the carriage, and an escort of two horsemen in front and two behind. The King rides in an eight-horse carriage, preceded and followed by twelve horsemen. People of rank, including princes, do not consider it beneath their dignity to walk a mile or two in the streets and bazaars, either by day or night; armed with no more than a cane or walking stick they often go out on foot in ordinary clothes. In this respect they are the opposite of the rajas and wealthy men of India. The English consider the size and pomp of Indian retinues as a most absurd and useless expense and laugh at the Indian noblemen for being fools and blockheads. They say that if anyone in England were to appear with such a pompous retinue the bazaar urchins would hurl taunts and dirt and stones at them.

The moral code of every nation is singular in its identification of particular things as being sinful or unseemly. The better classes of England consider it sinful to use the expression 'God damn.' Though it is constantly on the tongues of the common people, who use it jocularly as well as in earnest, there are many learned and respectable men who have never uttered it, for it means 'May the curse of God fall on you,' a very strong curse indeed! Similarly, among Muslims the use of the expression '*Lanutoollah*' ['The curse of Allah on you'] is considered highly improper. Besides, pious Christians say that God's name should properly be used in prayer, and it is disrespectful to do so heedlessly on the street or in bazaars. Well-born Englishmen even consider it unseemly to talk ceaselessly while walking in bazaars or on streets.

Again, among the English middle and upper classes, it is considered very wrong of one to call another a liar or a thief. Honour requires that such a slur is answered with a challenge to a duel with pistols. If one of the parties refuses to fight he is declared a coward and taunted by high and low alike; he cannot show his face again among his companions. If a duel is fought and one of the combatants dies, the other is obliged to fly to a foreign country to avoid being tried and perhaps hanged for manslaughter. Truly, the English hold honour dearer than life.

Many people in England are inveterate gamblers. They may lose all their property and effects at the table, and as a result come to be accounted uncommonly foolish. But what is strange is that they continue on the same course, for it may happen that they also win at times and therefore determine to keep trying their luck, considering perhaps that it is not essentially different from trading by sea. There are a few who acquire riches by games of hazard, but how many more are ruined and sunk in penury!

CHAPTER XV

VILAYETI MISCELLANEA

If I were to describe all the inventions made in England I would need a very long life and many books to fill.

The water mill and the windmill are very useful technological innovations of the Firinghees. They are used to run crushing and husking mills, sawmills, oil presses and gunpowder factories. I understand such mills have lately been set up in Calcutta. One can readily imagine how much the public is benefited from these labour-saving inventions. In a flour mill powered in this manner it is not unusual to ground fifty to a hundred maunds a day, or even more. Villagers can take wheat to be ground in these mills whenever they wish, as long as they pay the fixed charge per maund. Similar mills are there for pressing oil.

I saw spinning mills where a single operator turns a large wheel whose motion is automatically transferred to about twenty other wheels, which produce long silken yarns.

A brewery is an interesting factory to visit. From barley water it produces beer, which is a popular drink with rich and poor alike and is said to be cool and refreshing. Water raised from a well is used to fill huge vats in which a couple of thousand maunds of barley are boiled. Horses are used to raise the water in the following manner. Blinkered horses are yoked to a pole whose other end is fixed to a vertical axle attached to a wheel. When goaded the horse cannot but walk around the well, thereby causing the wheel to rotate. Since the wheel is attached to a rope with a bucket or waterskin at its end, the rotation raises water, which is then collected in a reservoir. I had learned from hearsay as well as from books that this method of raising water had been developed in ancient Iran and Turkestan, but it was in Vilayet that I first saw it in use.

Chronometers of various kinds can be seen in Vilayet. The most widely used are the pocket-watches, which all but the very poor carry. Then there are wall clocks, which are quite large, and are hung on the kitchen walls of the wealthy so that the cook may know by looking at it if it is time to prepare a meal; and in parks and bazaars, at the entrance of large buildings and in gardens, there are sundials. These comprise a circular stone or bronze face with markings indicating the different hours, and a dial in the centre, whose shadow on the markings indicates the hour of the day. In India the wealthy citizens employ gong-beaters to signal the different hours, but in Vilayet people of all classes keep track of time.

Food:
How can I enumerate all the things to eat and drink that can be procured in England, for (to borrow an expression):

> 'If you want fowl's milk, you can get it there.'

Flowers:
Though there is a great variety of flowers in India and Persia, I was quite impressed by those I saw in Vilayet. Among them were the tuberose, rose, the cockscomb flower, tulip, marigold, narcissus, *gool mhendee, nafurman, beli, mograh, jui and chameli*, besides a large number of white, red, yellow and blue flowers whose names I do not know. There was one flower, called the carnation, concerning which I recollect the following couplet in praise of a mistress:

> The rose is red, the violet's blue;
> Carnation's sweet, and so are you.

It was in England that I saw the largest roses in the world, growing in thousands.

Transport over long distances:
At every stage the traveller finds an inn, where he can rest and obtain meat and drink for himself, and corn and hay for horses. If he wishes he can cook his own food, and even procure the services of a courtesan.

There are stagecoaches, which change horses every ten or twelve miles and travel continuously both day and night, so that one has to make do with whatever rest or sleep one can get in the coach. In a day and a night, therefore, a coach can cover about one hundred and fifty miles. It will stop at inns where meals are ready and waiting, for which the passengers are allowed only a quarter of an hour.

People can also hire single horses or a post-chaise, which is a large vehicle in which four passengers can travel sitting face to face. Both can be obtained at inns. Of course those in very indigent circumstance are forced to walk.

Agriculture:
Vilayet is so intensively cultivated that there isn't a yard of ground on which crops are not raised. In my travels in England and Scotland I didn't see a single uncultivated tract large enough for an army of ten or twelve thousand, or indeed even of a thousand or five hundred men, to halt and set up camp.

The agricultural methods are quite different from India. The soil is seldom rich, and is generally poor and stony. The ground is first cleared by picking up the stones, then manured with horse and cow dung. Much labour is required to prepare it for planting, but in spite of this the farmers succeed in growing varieties of grain. In many places I saw a white soil, which is called 'chalk' in English; also a good deal of the red earth that Indians call *geroo*.

The ground is frost-bound for four months in the year, but in summer, when the sun enters Aries, is sufficiently warm to melt the ice and moisten the earth. Farmers now plough their fields using two-horse and four-horse ploughs, and sow barley and other crops. In four or five months the grain is ready for the sickle. Rain falls round the year, but there is only one crop, unlike India, where there are two, the *rabi* or winter crop, and the *khareef* or summer crop.

Animals:
In Vilayet horses cost less than in India, though they are twice as big as Indian horses and can do proportionately heavier work. The lower orders keep horses to draw carts and ploughs, and to carry loads. The work done in India by oxen, donkeys, camels, buffaloes and bullocks, is performed by horses alone. The English are amused

to hear that bullocks are used in India for riding, carrying burdens, and drawing carts. The roadsters and racehorses of Vilayet are not as fat as the other horses, and are very swift. Arab and Persian horses are held in great estimation, and fetch high prices.

Wild animals like tigers, wolves, leopards, bears, rock-snakes, serpents, lynxes and jackals are not to be seen in Vilayet. They say, however, that in bygone time the people were annoyed by many carnivorous and troublesome beasts. Therefore a number of men were appointed to scour the forests and hills and exterminate the animals, so that there is no vestige of them now. Only the sly fox survived by hiding in holes.

Here is a story illustrating the cunning of the fox. Once there lived a man who kept a large number of ducks. To ensure their safety at night he built a large wooden coop in which they were locked up. A fox had his eyes on the ducks and kept continuous nightly watch on the coop. At the end of one day the owner put the ducks into the coop, but forgot to lock the door, which remained open like the eyes of a lover, or the doors of the generous. The fox now had his chance. Quicker than wind or lightning, he entered the coop and pounced on the ducks' necks, so that they couldn't let out a squeak.

He then carried off the ducks to a sandy spot at a distance, buried them and smoothed the ground over them, thus providing himself with a store of provisions.

(O Allah! What foresight do these European foxes have. Whereas we alas, neither lay up a store for this life nor for the next!) In the morning, when the owner came to let out the ducks, he found to his amazement that the door was open, the coop empty, and no sign of his ducks. He raised a party to look for them in every direction. At last they came upon the communal grave of the birds, where they noticed a feather sticking out of the ground. They tugged at it and pulled out a dead bird. Then they dug up the ground and found the whole flock. The owner was very sorrowful at what happened.

Animals like elephants and camels are sent to Vilayet from India, and are kept in large buildings. The people of Vilayet consider them very extraordinary creatures and flock from near and far to see them. An entrance fee of one or two rupees is charged from each of them at the gate of the building.

The dogs of Vilayet are greatly celebrated, for they are taught to perform many wonderful and surprising tricks, about which the common people of India are utterly incredulous.

I saw dogs of many breeds and sizes. Among them the pointer particularly astonished me. One day I went out shooting on the plain outside Edinburgh with the son of a Mr. Sargeant and a gardener. It was autumn, when the wheat and barley are harvested. Mr. Sargeant took along a small pointer which we followed at a little distance. The dog hunted about in every direction for game, which he tried to sniff out, but for a long time had no success. Then, all at once, we came upon a field in which, unbeknownst to us, were ten or twelve partridges feeding in the grass. The moment the dog scented them he stopped dead in his tracks, at a distance of twenty cubits from them. He looked towards his master, then bowed his head. Mr. Sargeant knew at once that he was pointing at game. He advanced quickly, but failing to find any birds, he glanced angrily at the dog, which advanced ten paces and stood still again, for he well knew that his master was displeased with him at not seeing the game, and perhaps said to himself, 'My master thinks I am deceiving him.' Mr. Sargeant went forward, but still couldn't see anything. He therefore darted another angry glance at the dog, which again advanced. Mr. Sargeant followed, and yet there was no sign of the game, for they were among the wheat stubble, which was high enough to hide them completely. The master now flew into a rage and the pointer, fearing for his life, ran in upon the game. The covey immediately rose. Mr. Sargeant fired and brought down a brace of birds, and the gardener shot down a third. Mr. Sargeant knew that Muslims do not eat meat that has not been ritually sacrificed, so he brought the three partridges to me and asked me to sacrifice them. After I had done so he gave them all to me.

I found the meat very tasteful and savoury. Captain Swinton, on hearing that we had bagged some partridges and also how they had been disposed of, said in a bad humour, 'You could have given me one or two of them, for they are eaten by our caste.' I replied, 'If I had known that, I would have sent you all three.'

Larger breeds of dogs are used for the aristocratic pastimes of hunting foxes and hares. Truly, there is a great resemblance between the natures of dogs and men, which is evident from the way dogs hunt.

A number of businessmen in partnership set up kennels where they breed and train as many as four or five hundred hounds, which are hired out for fifty to one hundred rupees per week. When a hunt is organised, fifty to one hundred men get together and subscribe to pay for the hounds. They ride out to the fields with the dogs, which are in the charge of a mounted huntsman who carries a horn. The pack is set loose, and the hunt is on; the dogs separate and beat about in the jungle and on the common in search of game. When the huntsman blows his horn they leave off the search and gather round him; at another sign they return to the search. When they scent a fox or a hare in its lair, they begin digging the ground with their nails, on seeing which the horsemen gallop to the spot. If the hounds catch a deer in its sleep they will pounce on it, and if the deer escapes they will give it chase, followed by the hunters. Even if a deer has left a spot hours before the dogs can follow their scent, with the hunters galloping after, till at last they catch the prey. In this manner the hunters may gallop for twenty to twenty-five miles without a thought. They will not even pause a moment to catch their breath, and if they come across a ditch or a wall or fence as high as a man's height, they will clear it without ado.

It is now clear to me why aristocratic and wealthy Englishmen teach their children to ride from the age of four, and to exercise regularly on horseback till old age. They admire physical prowess and endurance, and despise indolence, slackness and indulgence in luxury. If such people do not extend their empire over many lands, who will – our present-day Indian emirs and princes, who gorge themselves on pilau, drink ice-cooled water, recline effeminately on soft velvet cushions and let luxury and self-indulgence rule their lives? And is it surprising if a country whose soldiers and noblemen are affected, luxurious and effeminate is subdued by a brave warlike people?

The person who strikes with his sword, his name becomes current.
Oh my life, a conceited man is not ornamented by ambition.
Those people only, who are brave and enterprising, keep their feet on this plain.

A Ring from Herculaneum:

In the ancient Roman empire there was a city called Herculaneum which is supposed to have been founded by a great hero called Hercules, who was revered like the Hindu avatars. The city was at the foot of a mountain, which contained a sulphur mine from which balls of fire erupted from tine to time. Once they fell on the city itself, burying it in a gigantic ash-heap. About two hundred years ago the people of the region excavated the city from the ash-heap and found everything in it intact – its houses built of stone and wood; its shops, stocked with merchandise; its streets, on which the wheel-tracks of chariots could be clearly seen. Even now ancient artefacts are being dug up there. A certain Mr. John David showed me a ring set with a ruby which his grandfather is said to have found in the ruins of Herculaneum.

My Hookah in England:
The various kinds of hookah we have in India are unknown in Vilayet, as well as in Turkey, Syria, Iran, Turan and China. In these countries tobacco is smoked in small pipes, and it is supposed to be good for colds and coughs. But in Vilayet the use of chewing tobacco is more popular among both rich and poor. I had taken along an ornamented hookah, which aroused such curiosity and wonderment that people came from afar to seem smoking it. They were intrigued by its gurgling sound which they thought was caused by something moving inside it, and I had to explain what actually happened.

CHAPTER XVI

THE RETURN

Differences of opinion between Captain Swinton and myself gradually put our relationship under strain. At the root of the problem lay Lord Clive's detestable breach of trust, as a consequence of which the Mughal Badshah's letter to the English King was never delivered and Clive's assurances to the Badshah came to nothing. It also affected Captain Swinton's career by ruining his hopes of returning to India.

But there were more immediate reasons for our deteriorating relationship. As I have already said, at this time there was none in England who knew the Persian language well, but many were eager to learn it. Captain Swinton, Doctor Fulton, Captain Steel and a number of other well-placed persons consulted among themselves and determined to keep me in their country for a few more years. On the group's behalf, Captain Swinton repeatedly tried to tempt me to stay on.

'At present there is no one in England who knows Persian well,' he said. 'Therefore many eminent men are eager to study the language under you, and they will be able to advance your interests. A remittance will be regularly sent to Bengal for the support of your wife and children, and should you, in accordance with your religions tenets, wish to have a second or even a third wife during your stay here, even that can be arranged.'

At first I took such words to be spoken in jest, and made no reply. But when his importunities exceeded all bounds, giving way to taunts and aspersions on my faith, religion and native mores, and most painful of all, attempts to compel me to accompany him on long trips and to share his food, I began to fear that I could not rely on the Captain's continued friendship and civility. Therefore I too cast off my sense of delicacy, refused to accept any more allowance from him, and began to retort in a manner consistent with my religious tenets. I said, 'I would much rather live in poverty in my own country than in affluence in yours, and to me the dusky Indian women are dearer than the fairy-faced Firinghee damsels.'

Captain Swinton still didn't give up entirely. He said, 'I intend to travel, and would like to take you with me. We will visit the different countries of Europe, where the experience of seeing many curiosities and spectacles will be instructive for us both.'

Actually, the true reason behind Captain Swinton's invitation was that ignorant people, seeing me in my Indian gentleman's costume, would take me for a nobleman, perhaps a Nawab's brother, and would infer that since Captain Swinton had brought me as a travelling companion he must have risen to great eminence in Bengal. In fact, I knew that the Captain's reputation had already been enhanced in this manner in Edinburgh and the surrounding countryside.

I said in reply, 'I too would like to travel in many countries, but I can do so only if my servant accompanies me to cook my food.'

Captain Swinton raised economic objections. 'You and I can travel in one carriage' he said. 'If we take your servant he'll have to come in a separate carriage, which will be very expensive. It's best if he remains here, and you and I eat together on the journey.'

This was quite unacceptable to me. I said, 'It goes directly against the principles of Islam to sacrifice religion for the sake of the world. You have shown me great kindness, but I must beg you to excuse me from going with you.'

Captain Swinton rejoined with a touch of irritation: 'I happen to know the Islamic precepts in this regard, and they permit a traveller to do whatever necessity compels him to do for survival, even if it violates mensal rules.'

'But I'm free not to undertake the travels,' I protested. 'The question of being compelled by necessity arises only if one is in bondage or faces death by starvation, in which case one may without disgrace eat whatever is at hand. But the doctors of our religion say that it is praiseworthy to refrain from violating the *Sharia* laws to attain worldly advantage, and it is noble to sacrifice one's life for the sake of the faith'.

Arguments of this sort were frequent. The Captain must have thought I was being foolish and bigoted, and would come round if I was forced to fast for a couple of days. Soon he got a chance to put me to trial, which caused me great hardship for a fortnight, though with the help of Providence I came through without suffering any harm.

This is what happened. A case had come up for trial in London against certain members of the East India Company's Calcutta Council, among them one Mr. John Johnstone, who was accused of having taken bribes from Nawab Mir Zafar Ali Khan, Muhammad Reza Khan, Maharaja Nand Kumar and Maharaja Rai Durlabh Ram. Captain Swinton, Captain Steel and Mr. Peacock, having lately returned from Bengal, were summoned as witnesses. With the intention of forcing me to accompany him to London Captain Swinton said, 'I have some Persian letters with me, which I shall need to substantiate my evidence. Therefore it is imperative that you come with me in order to read and translate them before the court.'

I tried to excuse myself on the plea that I would be greatly inconvenienced without my servant to cook my meals, but Captain Swinton was adamant. 'If we want to take your servant,' he said, 'we'll have to hire another carriage, and that may take five or six days. But I have been ordered to appear in court within three days. Therefore I must request you come alone.'

What could I do? I surrendered to fate, and preparing to face death, got into the carriage with the Captain. I took with me only my hookah and some tobacco.

After travelling continuously for a day and a night we stopped at an inn, where I prepared some sherbet to drink and finished my dinner with a few almonds, raisins and dates. When the Captain's dinner was served, he sent for me and said, 'This meal consists of wheaten bread, which both our peoples eat, and fowl and mutton, but none of the flesh forbidden to your people. Our way of killing animals isn't different from yours, either. You cut through the skin and half the neck, while we pierce the throat to take out the blood and then sever the head and neck, but we never eat an animal that has died a natural death. Then why do you refuse to eat this meat? Why do you behave like the blockheads of Calcutta and bring suffering on yourself?'

I replied: 'You too are people of the book, for which reason we are in fact permitted to eat food cooked by your people, provided they are clean and the utensils are free of impurities, and, above all, if the meat has been sacrificed by a Muslim. For, merely cutting the throat doesn't make a sacrifice. Ablutions must be performed and a prayer to Allah offered, which cannot be done by one who isn't a Muslim. Besides, you cook without salt, spices or ghee, so that the offensive odour of raw meat is not dispelled from the meat. How can I swallow such food?'

While I was making this speech, the Captain knitted his brows. At last he said, 'You Muslims think we are filthy eaters.'

I said at once, 'I had no intention to imply that, or to insult you. I merely wish to say that each nation has its own peculiar customs and practices, and so the food of one country will be pleasant to the taste of its natives, but to foreigners it may be unpalatable. We should remember in particular that between your manners and customs and ours there is the difference of east and west.'

While we were carrying on this conversation the flames of hunger raged in my stomach. The few almonds and other things I had eaten with the sherbet merely whetted my appetite, which was now doubly keen.

When we arrived in London I felt so faint from weariness and hunger that until the second watch of the day I lay like a corpse, unable to make the slightest movement. Captain Swinton's servant discovered me in this condition, and fearing the worst, ran to inform his master, who rushed nervously to my bedside and began calling my name, which roused me from my trance. When he asked after my health I replied that I was well enough, though very weak. He at once ordered his servant to bring me rice, spices and a chicken. I sacrificed the chicken, cooked a curry and boiled some rice, and after eating slept till evening. The next morning I was my old self again. During the week we spent in London I cooked my own meals. Four of us then took a coach and returned to Edinburgh in five days.

On another occasion Captain Swinton took me to a town in the Highlands, where his elder brother John was chief Magistrate. It was one day's journey from Edinburgh. The whole trip took three days and nights, during which time I was reduced to the same sorry plight as in London.

One day Captain Swinton said to me: 'I spent twenty years in

Bengal, during which time I became well acquainted with the manners of Muslims. I have lived with Nawabs and the sons of emirs and shared their food and drink. I observed that they would abstain from alcohol in the presence of strangers, proclaiming loudly, "We never drink wine"; but as soon as they were by themselves they would snatch the goblet from the cup-bearer, and guzzling copiously, declare, "Wine is an excellent thing, a divine blessing without an equal on earth. Muslims are forbidden to drink before people, but to do so in private is quite in order." Now, you are a stranger in this country and none of your countrymen will know of your doings, yet you neither eat our meat nor drink our wine. The only reason I can think of for this is that you are a Bengali, and the Bengalis are notorious among Indians for their folly and stupidity.'

I replied: 'Among Muslims true nobility is not measured by worldly wealth but consists in acquiring knowledge, in leading an upright life, and in obeying the laws of Allah and his prophet. If pride of wealth or the devil's temptations prompts any person of rank to act contrary to his religious precepts, he is definitely culpable, and therefore there is no reason why a Muslim of humble rank should follow his example. What, in any case, are worldly riches worth? To our religious leaders a righteous and faithful beggar is superior to the irreligious son of a prophet. Everybody curses the Pharaoh, who was a wealthy king, because he disregarded the injunctions of Hazrat Musa, and so it is wicked of the common people to follow the irreligious out of a hankering after worldly wealth, or to neglect their religion in order to please powerful but impious people.

'Among us Muslims poverty is not considered disgraceful. On the contrary, it is honourable, because our prophet and his companions deemed even a beggar's wooden slipper of equal worth to a royal crown. They kicked aside worldly property and wealth, and their descendants, being of the same way of thinking, are not ashamed of poverty, and consider religion far more important than sublunary matters. To the wealthy and to foreigners the religious poor may seem miserable and contemptible, but Muslim kings and nobles have always respected and honoured them. All this can be confirmed from chronicles and history books.

'My ancestors were Sayyids, or descendants of the Prophet, and some of them were of the families of the Prophet's companions.

Assuredly, then, they were heirs to the Caliphate, and had a claim to the crown and throne. But they gave up worldly honours from a love of prayer and a desire for acquiring knowledge, and lived in retirement on what people willingly gave them. The Sultans of India and the Turkish Caliph gave them pensions and *jagirs*, or freehold property. When the children of the Sayyids began to increase, and spread through Persia and India, Rajas and emperors showed them great honour and favour, but also reflected uneasily: "These people know they have a rightful claim to the Caliphate and to kingly power, and will perhaps foment war and strife." As a precaution many rulers (But not the Moghuls) lowered the rank and status of the Sayyids, so that when over the generations their number greatly increased and they had little to subsist on, they began to look for service, often travelling far and wide to solicit the favour of the opulent. Thanks and praise be to Allah, that to this day they are generally firmly attached to their religion. I am a poor man of Sayyid descent, who have been allured by the prospect of gain to travel to this country. Forlorn and friendless, subjected to continual hardship and unable to help myself, I must patiently wait the issue.

Though the head of Zecheriah was sawn asunder, he made no complaint,
Though misfortune befall the sons of Adam, they will in time get over them.

Captain Swinton felt the sincerity in my words. Still, as is always the case among his countrymen, who condemn the poor and consider the rich illustrious, he couldn't accept everything that I said and continued to argue with me. But in my absence he would praise me to his acquaintances, saying, 'In all the time I spent in Bengal I never saw such a strict Muslim as this man is. On the voyage he had a severe attack of diarrhoea, which made me fear for his life. I was very anxious to administer a draught of wine, by way of medicine, but he wouldn't touch a drop and recovered without it.'

One day Captain Swinton asked me, 'What is the secret of your good health?'

'Abstinence,' I replied. 'When I set out for Vilayet I was anxious on account of the temptations that lay in wait for me. I therefore prayed to Allah, "O Lord! Preserve me from drinking wine," and then onwards led a very temperate life, for I know that if I fell ill the English doctors would prescribe wine as a tonic. The Almighty has compassionately answered my prayer and kept me in good health.'

I remained in Vilayet one year and six months, all this time expecting the Moghul Emperor's letter. But when Lord Clive eventually returned to England he presented the Emperor's gift to the English King in his own name, thereby obtaining an abundant share of royal favour, and made no mention of the letter. Neither did Captain Swinton open his mouth regarding it, out of friendship for his lordship, on whose promises of favour he placed great reliance. But he was distressed at Clive's deviousness and said to me, 'What you feared has come to pass – Lord Clive has completely deceived me.' But Lord Clive was being covered by the company's directors and without connections among the King's ministers Captain Swinton could not have exposed him even if he had wanted to.

Some time after I discovered the reason why Badshah Shah Alam's letter had been suppressed. At that time there was a dispute between the King's ministers and the Company regarding the conquest of Bengal and a few other matters. The minister argued that the Company were only agents and merchants, and therefore did not have the right to conquer a country. They claimed that the conquest was the result of the efforts and sacrifices of Royal troops, and the administration of the country should consequently be in the hands of the King's government; meanwhile the Company should be employed solely in trade. The Company rejoined that during the wars with Nawab Siraj-ud-Dowla and Nawab Mir Kasim Ali Khan their factories in Bengal had been plundered, causing losses amounting to crores of rupees. Besides, they spent large sums in paying and maintaining the troops, and it was solely owing to the company's officers, who worked tirelessly in the face of many hardships, that Bengal was conquered. The Company was paying such tribute and taxes to the King as it was bound to according to an existing agreement; the ministers by their arguments were opposing this compact and hence deviating from their characteristic uprightness.

The dispute continued, but it became clear that the ministers couldn't substantiate their claims with either convincing arguments or unimpeachable documents. Lord Clive, being a well-wisher of the Company, after consulting with the Directors, thought it expedient to suppress the Badshah's letter, which would have materially helped the ministers' cause.

I came to know of these happenings after my return to India. The dispute continued for three years, at the end of which it was referred to the King for arbitration. The King wisely pronounced: 'The Badash of India, Shah Alam, has given Bengal to the Company as a gift. If we bring it under our administration we shall in effect be receiving the Badshah's patronage, and our position will be akin to that of a tributary. This would be a humiliation for us, especially now that the whole of India has come under the sway of British arms.' After this pronouncement ended the dispute, the King's ministers levied a tax of several crore rupees on the Company, together with the provision of an annual increase. Some say that both parties have agreed that after a few years the Company will hand over the government of Bengal to the King's ministers, but Allah alone knows if there is any truth in this.

Captain Swinton tried everything he could to induce me to stay on for another three or four years. But I could not but decline, being so depressed at my separation from my native land and friends that I cared little about acquiring riches or temporal advantages.

One's homeland is dearer than Solomon's throne!
The thorns of one's native land are sweeter than fragrant blossoms in a strange country!
Even Joseph, who was given to rule Egypt, used to say – I'd rather be a beggar in Canaan

At last Captain Swinton gave me in the charge of Mr. Michaund, who was formerly chief secretary to the Council in Calcutta, and bade me farewell. I returned to Bengal in 1769. I had spent a whole year aboard ship for the round trip, one year in England and Scotland, seven months in Madras, and two months at different ports of call, which comes to two years and nine months for the entire trip.

For being permitted to return safely to my native country I gave praise and thanks to the Almighty.

FINIS

INDEX